# Langland's Fictions

# LANGLAND'S FICTIONS

J. A. BURROW

CLARENDON PRESS · OXFORD
1993

Oxford University Press, Walton Street, Oxford OX2 6DP
Oxford New York Toronto
Delhi Bombay Calcutta Madras Karachi
Kuala Lumpur Singapore Hong Kong Tokyo
Nairobi Dar es Salaam Cape Town
Melbourne Auckland Madrid
and associated companies in
Berlin Ibadan

Oxford is a trade mark of Oxford University Press

Published in the United States
by Oxford University Press Inc., New York

© J. A. Burrow 1993

British Library Cataloguing in Publication Data
Data available

Library of Congress Cataloging in Publication Data

Burrow, J. A. (John Anthony)
Langland's fictions / J. A. Burrow.
Revision of four Alexander Lectures delivered in Toronto in 1989.
Includes bibliographical references and index.
1. Langland, William, 1330? – 1400? Piers the Plowman.
2. Christian poetry, English (Middle)—History and criticism.
3. Dreams in literature. I. Title.
PR2017.D73B87 1993 821'.1—dc20 92–26820 CIP
ISBN 0–19–811293–9

Typeset by Pure Tech Corporation, Pondicherry, India
Printed in Great Britain
on acid-free paper by Bookcraft Ltd.,
Midsomer Norton, Bath

# Acknowledgements

The four main chapters of this book are revised versions of four Alexander Lectures delivered in Toronto in the autumn of 1989. I am grateful to the University of Toronto for the honour of its invitation to deliver the 1989 Alexander Lectures, and to the Principal of University College, Toronto, and his colleagues for their generous hospitality. Professor John Leyerle, in particular, and also Patricia Eberle, Richard Green, and George and Jennifer Rigg, were among those who helped to make my visit a most memorable and happy one. Versions of the lecture upon which Chapter 4 is based have also been delivered in Alcala de Henares and in Hakone, and as the 1991 Byron Foundation Lecture at the University of Nottingham. I owe a further debt of gratitude to the Oxford University Press for undertaking the publication of a rather short book.

Since this study is chiefly concerned with the B Text of *Piers Plowman*, passages quoted without assignment to a particular version are to be understood as coming from B: A. V. C. Schmidt (ed.), *William Langland, The Vision of Piers Plowman: A Complete Edition of the B-Text*, revised edition (London, 1987). For the A Text I quote from George Kane (ed.), *Piers Plowman: The A Version* (London, 1960), and for the C Text from Derek Pearsall (ed.), *Piers Plowman, by William Langland: An Edition of the C-Text* (London, 1978). I make no use of the Z Text— *William Langland, Piers Plowman: The Z Version*, ed. A. G. Rigg and Charlotte Brewer (Toronto, 1983)—since its differences from the A Text are of little interest to this particular study.

Quotations from the Bible are taken from the Vulgate Latin and from the English Douai versions.

J.A.B.

# Contents

# Abbreviations

AV      The Authorized Version of the Bible
EETS    The Early English Text Society
*MED*   *Middle English Dictionary*
*MLN*   *Modern Language Notes*
*PL*    *Patrologia Latina*
*RES*   *Review of English Studies*

# Introduction

William Langland's *Piers Plowman* is a poem which has always had a particular appeal for those readers who share, in one form or another, the poet's own Christian faith. Thus, in our own time, many of the poem's best scholars and critics have been Roman Catholics. Something of what Langland's work might mean to such readers is suggested by the words of the late J. A. W. Bennett: 'Though *Piers Plowman* has been read and circulated for six hundred years, its position as the supreme English testament of Christian faith and practice has still to be recognized . . . Had the fifteenth-century Church taken heed to it, England might still have been a Catholic country: the popular religion, tinged with superstition, and the intellectual slackness that "played into the hands of Protestant critics" have no place in Langland's poem.'[1] This statement is no doubt enough in itself to justify all the time and attention that Bennett devoted to the poem, as editor and interpreter; but it may also prompt other Langlandians who are not believers to ask themselves how they justify their own preoccupation with this 'supreme English testament of Christian faith'. On what terms does it survive, or transcend, their incredulity? What does it mean to them?

No doubt the many unbelieving admirers of *Piers Plowman* would have a variety of differing stories to tell about their relationship with this peculiarly gripping poem. In my own case—and I speak as an unbeliever—I was first gripped by certain strong lines and passages. Thus I remember being struck by the pun on 'head' in a line about the knowledge of love, 'And in the herte, there is the heed and the heighe welle', and also by the sublime strangeness of lines such as 'Feddest tho with thi fresshe blood oure forefadres in derknesse' and 'Til the vendage falle in the vale of Josaphat'. Langland, I at once saw, was a poet capable of remarkable writing, unlike anything I had read elsewhere. But, as I got

[1] J. A. W. Bennett, *Poetry of the Passion: Studies in Twelve Centuries of English Verse* (Oxford, 1982), 85.

to know the poem better, I began also to appreciate another source of its peculiar power: the poet's ability to create imaginary figures and scenes, dream-fictions and allegories, that haunt the mind. Hence the subject of the present study: the imaginary worlds of *Piers Plowman*.

This topic has, for infidels, the obvious advantage of directing attention away from those aspects of the poem that raise questions of religious belief. Yet such an emphasis upon the imaginary and the fictional may perhaps seem inappropriate or even perverse in the case of *Piers Plowman*. Unlike his contemporary Chaucer, Langland strikes one as a poet intensely concerned with truth—the truth about his faith, his society, and himself. His poem addresses real-life questions concerning salvation, social reform, and the like, often with an unapologetic directness foreign to the author of *Troilus and Criseyde* and *The Canterbury Tales*. There are occasions when it seems that Langland forgets all about his dream-fiction, the literal level of his allegory, and addresses himself directly *in propria persona* to us or to some section of his contemporaries: 'Forthi biddeth noght, ye beggeres, but if ye have gret nede.' Indeed one critic, Rosemary Woolf, has gone so far as to speak generally of Langland's 'indifference to the literal level of his allegory', characterizing it as 'tenuous and confused', 'slight and poetically unimportant'.[2]

Few lovers of *Piers Plowman* will deny that it has stretches where its literal level is indeed tenuous and slight. Certainly this charge holds against the extended sequence in B Text Passus VIII–X, where Long Will's search for knowledge of Dowel leads him to be instructed in turn by Thought, Wit, Study, Clergy, and Scripture. Here Langland's fictive imagination asserts itself only sporadically, and most readers remember little more than a succession of didactic speeches. Yet in the poem as a whole, I shall argue, a fictive imagination is powerfully at work. The literal level, though it may sometimes be confused, is far from being 'poetically unimportant'.

In the first chapter, I consider *Piers Plowman* as a dream poem, and emphasize particularly Langland's art in construct-

---

[2] 'Some Non-Medieval Qualities of *Piers Plowman*', in Rosemary Woolf, *Art and Doctrine: Essays on Medieval Literature*, ed. Heather O'Donoghue (London, 1986), 85–97; 91, 86, 85. The essay was first published in *Essays in Criticism*, 12 (1962), 111–25.

ing it out of a number of separate dreams—in the B Text, no less than ten. This manner of construction was something of a novelty in the tradition of medieval dream poetry. It may be regarded as the formal manifestation of that 'lack of a sustained literal level' to which Miss Woolf also referred as a general characteristic of the poem.[3] Certainly Langland does not sustain a single, continuous narrative throughout Will's dreams—as did Guillaume de Lorris, say, in the single dream of the *Roman de la Rose*. Yet the narrative discontinuity of *Piers Plowman* should not be ascribed to any mere 'indifference' on Langland's part towards the coherence of his dream-worlds. Thus, the endings of most of the individual dreams are skilfully calculated to furnish both the end of one story and the cue for the next, so that the whole hangs together as a complex 'poly-narrative'.

In this respect, as in others, Langland's fictive imagination works in harmony with his mind—a restless mind, which has been aptly characterized by invoking T. S. Eliot's words, 'That was a way of putting it—not very satisfactory'. His multiple, discontinuous dream structure allows him, as it were, to try out 'ways of putting it'. Thus, in B XVI–XVIII the elusive essence of charity is suggested first by the emblem of the Tree of Charity, then by the parable of the Good Samaritan, and finally by a dream version of Christ's Passion. Elsewhere this same restlessness finds expression in certain 'fictions of the divided mind', discussed in my second chapter. Here it is Langland's sensitivity to conflicting considerations and apparently irreconcilable truths that is particularly in question. In the best of these, the poem creates an imaginary space within which the irreconcilables can coexist in some kind of precariously just equilibrium. Thus, many passages in *Piers* display a divided mind about the importance of learned and intellectual activities to the Christian life. Such activities have a part to play, evidently; but they can also, evidently, be a dangerous distraction. I argue that Langland handles this particular dilemma best, not in general discussions such as that of Imaginatif, but in the scene of leave-taking between Clergy and Conscience at the end of the dinner party in B XIII. The

---

[3] Ibid. 86.

pros and cons of the learned activities that Clergy represents are balanced one against the other in this confrontation, with a delicacy that seems beyond the powers of abstract argument. This is one of the uses of fiction in Langland's poem.

Another function is performed by what I call, in Chapter 3, 'fictions of history'. In the latter part of *Piers Plowman*, from a point in Passus XVI onwards to the end of the poem, the action loosely follows the order of history: the history of salvation, passing from Old Testament times through the life of Christ to the subsequent history of the Church. It might seem that Langland is here abandoning fiction for history; yet the rendering of biblical and postbiblical scenes here never approaches the plain literal manner of such biblical-para-phrase poems as the *Stanzaic Life of Christ*. Rather, Langland incorporates biblical events into the imaginary world of his poem, often to very bold effect. Thus, in Will's dreams of the life of Christ he sees Christ receiving instruction from a creature of the poet's own imagination, Piers Plowman, and wearing at the Entry into Jerusalem armour borrowed from Piers. So even Christ becomes, for the purposes of the poem, subject to the laws of fiction and the exigencies of art. Langland did not, I am sure, for a moment doubt the historical truth of the Gospels; rather, by recycling Gospel events in the dreaming of Will, he brings them to bear directly upon the condition of modern man—as when Will, after waking from his dream of the Resurrection, rises and attends Easter mass.

The title of my fourth chapter, 'Fictions of Self?', carries a question-mark, because it is here much less easy to trace the processes by which waking realities are transmuted into the stuff of poetic dream. In the case of salvation-history, we know what the realities were (for Langland, that is); but how could we ever discover the realities of the poet's own self? I argue, however, that there is in practice—whatever may be the case in theory—no way of reading the poem that does not involve some commitment, one way or the other, on the 'autobiographical question'. To what extent, if at all, is the figure of Long Will the dreamer to be read as authorial self-portraiture, reflecting Langland's own circumstances and self-doubts? I suggest my answer to this impossible question through readings of three passages where Will is subjected to criticism and offers, or is offered, excuses in self-defence—passages which I take as contributing to the poet's 'Self-Portrait as Long Will'. However, even if these passages represent, as I believe, Langland's troubled thinking about his own way of life, they are none the less also evident products of the fictive imagination. Perhaps, after all, the contradiction is only apparent. It may be said that we all, in real life, help to create our 'selves' by imagining them; and an author such as Langland, when he imagines himself in a poem such as *Piers Plowman*, under the special conditions of literary art, may be doing no less than just that: creating a 'fiction of self'.

# CHAPTER 1

# A Gathering of Dreams

*Piers Plowman* belongs to a species of medieval poem now known as the 'dream poem' or 'dream vision'. It is something of a mystery why this genre should have flourished particularly in the later Middle Ages. In France there was, among many others, the *Roman de la Rose*, and in the fourteenth century its religious counterpart, the three *Pelerinages* of Guillaume de Deguileville. English poets followed suit: Chaucer, in *The Book of the Duchess, The House of Fame, The Parlement of Foules*, and the Prologue to *The Legend of Good Women*; the *Gawain*-poet in *Pearl*; and Langland in *Piers Plowman*. It was not uncommon for these writers to introduce into their work some reflections on dreams and their interpretation—Chaucer does this at the beginning of *The House of Fame*, Langland in the epilogue to his second dream—but modern attempts to credit them with any sustained or serious effort at rendering actual dream experience have been only sporadically illuminating. When Langland introduces the hero of the Entry into Jerusalem not as Christ but as 'Oon semblable to the Samaritan, and somdeel to Piers the Plowman' (B XVIII. 10), one may be reminded of Freud's account of how dreams conflate or 'condense' disparate figures from waking experience into a single 'composite person' of questionable identity;[1] but such moments are rather rare, and there seems little point in celebrating every oddity and surprise in these poems as a triumph of dream-realism.

A better way of looking at the matter is to see the dream form as offering the medieval writer a kind of relief from his culture's insistent demand for literal truth.[2] A dream poet

---

[1] 'For purposes of dream-condensation I may construct a *composite person* . . . by combining the actual features of two or more persons in a single dream-image', *The Interpretation of Dreams*, in *The Basic Writings of Sigmund Freud*, ed. A. A. Brill (New York, 1938), 328. For discussion of dream-work in *Piers*, see Constance B. Hieatt, *The Realism of Dream Visions: The Poetic Exploitation of the Dream-Experience in Chaucer and his Contemporaries* (The Hague and Paris, 1967), ch. 7.

[2] See Jacqueline T. Miller, *Poetic License: Authority and Authorship in Medieval and Renaissance Contexts* (New York and Oxford, 1986), ch. 2, 'Dream Visions of *Auctorite*'.

could always claim one kind of documentary truth, inasmuch as he purports to record a dream which he actually had; and he could also, much more seriously, claim that the fantastic events of the dream contain deeper truths within them, to be recovered by the customary processes of dream-interpretation. Guillaume de Lorris makes the latter claim in his *Roman de la Rose*:

> La verité, qui est coverte,
> Vos sera lores toute overte
> Quant espondre m'oroiz le songe,
> Car il n'i a mot de mençonge.[3]

Yet Guillaume's rhyme between *songe* and *mençonge*, frequently employed by French poets of the time, suggests a contrary consideration. Events in dreams have not, in themselves, really happened, and dream people do not really exist; nor can the dream poet's claim to be rendering faithfully his night-time experience ever be subject to normal methods of verification. So the matter of dreams offered the narrative poet a kind of freedom that he could not hope to enjoy when treating, say, the traditional matters of Rome or Britain. Dream poems did, of course, develop their own generic conventions; but their narratives were free from the pressure, so persistent in medieval writing, to follow (however waveringly) the course laid down by 'olde stories'. Figures such as Gawain in *Sir Gawain and the Green Knight* or Troilus in *Troilus and Criseyde* are indeed creations of the fictive imagination—yet the imagination working within the wide boundaries of what was then considered historical truth; but the figure of Piers the Plowman is pure fictive *mençonge*.

No medieval poet took advantage of this rare freedom more boldly than did Langland. His invention—to use the old rhetorical term—positively runs riot, producing an extraordinary variety of imagined creations, some of them successful, some not. 'Originality' is not a term much favoured by modern studies of medieval literature; but I cannot believe that any amount of further research into Langland's sources

---

[3] Ed. Félix Lecoy, Classiques Français du Moyen Age (Paris, 1965–70), lines 2071–4: 'The truth which is hidden here will be made completely plain to you when you hear my exposition of the dream—for there is, in fact, not a lying word in it.'

and models will dispel the impression that *Piers Plowman* represents, in the tradition of dream poetry, a radically original development.

The present chapter will be chiefly concerned with one of the most striking of Langland's innovations. It was customary for dream poems to open with a dreamer falling asleep and end with his waking up. Thus the main body of the poem, apart from brief waking episodes at the beginning and end, would be devoted to the story of the dream – a single dream, that is, even in such very long works as the *Roman de la Rose*. *Piers Plowman*, on the other hand, presents a series of dreams, separated from each other by waking episodes. This structure is most clearly and fully articulated in the B Text, which has as many as ten dreams, including in that number (another innovation) two dreams-within-a-dream.[4] I know of only one precedent for this multiple structure, and that is in the work of Langland's French predecessor, Guillaume de Deguileville. Deguileville's three massive dream poems, *Le Pelerinage de Vie Humaine*, *Le Pelerinage de l'Ame*, and *Le Pelerinage de Jhesucrist*, were intended, as their common pilgrimage titles suggest, to form a trilogy; and some of the many manuscripts preserve them as a continuous sequence, with the three dreams linked by intervals of waking, much as in *Piers Plowman*. I argue in Appendix A that Langland did indeed know the French trilogy; but his waking interludes perform a function rather different from Deguileville's. The French dreams do, as the poet claims, 'depend upon' each other, especially the second upon the first;[5] but the three *Pelerinages* were nevertheless sufficiently distinct for them to be circulated separately, as Langland's dreams never were and never could have been. They form part of what could only be a single poem. Yet the

---

[4] R. W. Frank, 'The Number of Visions in *Piers Plowman*', *MLN* 66 (1951), 309–12. The A Text has the first three dreams only, with the third unfinished; the C Text has nine, with a mishandling of the second dream-within-a-dream, as Frank explains.

[5] In the introduction to the *Ame*: 'Un autre songe ressongai | Que cy apres vous compterai, | Et me semble que deppendant | Est de l'autre songe devant | Pour continuer le chemin | Dont fait estoie pelerin; | Car encor pas ne l'avoie | Acheve si com cuidoie.' ['I dreamed another dream, which I will tell you now. It follows, I think, from the previous dream, to continue the pilgrimage upon which I had set out; for I had not yet finished it as I expected to.'] *Le Pelerinage de l'Ame de Guillaume de Deguileville*, ed. J. J. Stürzinger, Roxburghe Club (London, 1895), lines 25–32.

waking interludes do play an important part in *Piers*, for they break the poem up into separate parts, each of which, though it will 'depend' upon its predecessor, can have its own integrity and prompt a fresh exercise of the fictive imagination. Thus Will's first dream brings the story of Lady Meed to a conclusion, and is followed by the dream of the pilgrimage to Truth—a story which, though it follows from what has gone before, exhibits a different narrative and symbolic structure. The third dream (Passus VIII–XII) is different again, centring on the dreamer's search for knowledge of Dowel; and it is followed in its turn by the story of Patience, confronting the Friar at Conscience's dinner party and then Hawkin on the road. And so on.

It will be evident, then, that the dream divisions introduce into Langland's poem an element of narrative discontinuity quite distinct from anything to be found in even the longest and most rambling of its predecessors. Structurally, indeed, *Piers* might even be compared to Italo Calvino's 'poly-novel', *If on a Winter's Night a Traveller*—a book in which, as Calvino puts it, 'a number of novels succeed one another and cross one another's paths.'[6]

This discontinuity produces, in the fictive worlds of the poem, some rather curious results. Thus, where the characters are concerned, one cannot safely make the normal assumption that a given name will necessarily, from one dream to another, denote the same person or personification. In the dream of the Harrowing of Hell, for instance, Langland introduces the traditional set of the 'Four Daughters of God', called Righteousness, Truth, Mercy, and Peace; but this Truth is not to be identified with the Truth of the first two dreams, who is no less than God himself, and this Peace has little more than her name in common with the Peace who figured in the story of Lady Meed.[7] They belong to different fictional worlds; and

[6] Italo Calvino, *The Literature Machine: Essays*, trans. Patrick Creagh (London, 1987), 203–4.
[7] Treating the two Peaces as one produces awkward results, as in this comment on the Peace of Passus IV: 'Peace is one of the Four Daughters of God in Passus XVIII; here, however, he[?] meekly accepts Meed's golden present in exchange for his broken head and lost wife—peace at any price, rather than the peace that passeth understanding', Mary J. Carruthers, *The Search for St. Truth: A Study of Meaning in 'Piers Plowman'* (Evanston, Ill., 1973), 47.

a composite list of Langland's dramatis personae would have to register two Truths and two Peaces.

The same discontinuity between dreams can on occasion produce more disturbing results, in cases where identity is not in doubt. Pure personifications present no problems in such cases. A figure such as Conscience, who appears in a number of dreams throughout the poem, will always represent whatever his name denotes—conscience, in some appropriate medieval sense of the term—and not even the most dedicated novel-reader should be tempted to reconstruct for him a personal history. Personifications properly have no history. They can neither recall the past nor anticipate the future, and they are incapable of change. In the confession scene in Passus V, the personifications of the deadly sins may resolve to amend; yet we know that Sloth, Glutton, and the rest cannot change their ways without ceasing to be what they are. The case is different, however, with the two most important actors in the poem: Piers Plowman and the dream-narrator himself, Long Will. These both have proper names—familiar forms of Peter and William, respectively—and names of that sort clearly mark them as something other than simple personifications. They are indeed represented as individual persons, albeit persons who can also function as symbols (in the case of Piers) or as personifications (in the case of Will). We might even call them characters. The result is that readers are tempted to treat them as if they were indeed characters in a continuous narrative, and to look for the kind of continuity that such a character should exhibit.[8] But Langland's discontinuous dream-world resists such readings.

I shall return to Long Will in the fourth chapter. As for Piers the Plowman, the peculiarity of this dream figure may best be suggested by looking at a place where Langland put a foot wrong—and later, I think, came to realize that he had

[8] The distinction between persons and personifications corresponds to that drawn by Roland Barthes between *personnages* and *figures*. The former exist in a 'durée biographique' and possess proper names: 'Le Nom propre fonctionne comme le champ d'aimantation [magnetic field] des sèmes; renvoyant virtuellement à un corps, il entraîne la configuration sémique dans un temps évolutif (biographique).' By contrast, the *figure*: 'ce n'est plus une combinaison de sèmes fixés sur un Nom civil, et la biographie, la psychologie, le temps ne peuvent plus s'emparer; c'est une configuration incivile, impersonelle, achronique, de rapports symboliques.' *S/Z* (Paris, 1970), 74.

done so. At the end of the pilgrimage to Truth in the second dream, after Piers has received Truth's pardon on behalf of the people, there follows in the A and B Texts a striking episode. Piers tears the pardon up, and resolves to live a different kind of life in future:

> 'I shal cessen of my sowyng,' quod Piers, 'and swynke noght
>     so harde,
> Ne aboute my bely joye so bisy be na moore;
> Of preieres and of penaunce my plough shal ben herafter,
> And wepen whan I sholde slepe, though whete breed me faille.'
> (B VII. 118–21)

This is not a case of Glutton swearing to give up drink. Piers is a person, or so his name implies, and his solemn speech of resolution projects a future for him which a reader will expect to be fulfilled; for in normal narratives, where continuity of character is taken for granted, utterances of this sort play a key part in establishing expectations of what is to come. This, one supposes, is how the character may be expected to develop; and if not, one will expect the failure to be itself meaningful. But *Piers Plowman* is not a normal narrative; and the expectations set up by Piers's speech of resolution turn out not to be fulfilled, in the event, nor indeed to be disappointed in any significant way. In the following dream, Piers plays no part at all; and he is not so much as mentioned until, some 1,700 lines later, Clergy cites 'oon Piers the Plowman' as an authority who sets love above learning:

> 'For oon Piers the Plowman hath impugned us alle,
> And set alle sciences at a sop save love one.'
> (XIII. 123–4)

The effect of this is unsettling. The once familiar figure of the plowman, almost forgotten after so long an interval, is now invoked as a mysterious and distant authority on the spiritual life—an authority to which even the clerisy defers. This is giving up ploughing with a vengeance. Indeed, it is hard to connect this Piers with his former self, the Piers who resolved to live a life of prayers and penance. The promise of that resolve is here fulfilled only in the loose sense that the new Piers is clearly a higher and more spiritual being than the plowman on the half acre. So Langland was surely wise to do what he did in the C Text, which was to cut Piers's speech of resolution out of the poem altogether. Looking back at B, he must have seen that the passage represented a false start. The Piers of the B and C Texts could not be understood in terms of such continuous character development, whatever the poet may have intended when he first wrote the speech.

Yet *Piers Plowman* is, of course, not a collection of separate poems. No scholar has ever proposed that it ought to be retitled *The Works of William Langland*. The dreams are formally distinct and each may tell a different story from its neighbours, but they form part of a greater whole and are, in fact, linked together in a variety of interesting ways. Since the idea of a sequence of dreams was itself quite new, Langland here faced certain new technical problems, in the articulation of his imaginary worlds. To suggest how he solved these problems, it is worth looking at the ways his dreams end.

Any completed literary dream, whether it is part of a sequence or not, must end with an awakening; and Langland evidently shared with other dream poets of his day an interest in that moment—the timing of it, and especially the motivating of it. When will the dreamer wake up, and why? The least interesting answer is that he wakes when the action of his dream is completed, and simply because it is completed. Jean de Meun concluded the *Roman de la Rose* in this flat fashion. Having achieved his rose, the dreamer just wakes up, in a single couplet:

> Ainsint oi la rose vermeille.
> Atant fu jorz, et je m'esveille.[9]

Langland himself achieves little more than this at the end of his first dream, where the story of Lady Meed has concluded in the triumph of Conscience and Reason at the king's court:

> The kyng and hise knyghtes to the kirke wente
> To here matyns of the day and the masse after.
> Thanne waked I of my wynkyng and wo was withalle
> That I ne hadde slept sadder and yseighen moore.
>
> (V. 1–4)

---

[9] Ed. Lecoy, lines 21749–50.

Like the return of the hunters from the forest at the end of Chaucer's *Book of the Duchess*, the departure of the king and his retinue from Westminster Hall (where the case of Lady Meed has been heard) creates a definite sense of an ending. However, Langland employs this same departure motif more brilliantly and enigmatically much later in the poem, when he comes to conclude his ninth dream. At this point, Conscience has summoned the people to his eucharistic feast in the barn of Holy Church, laying down certain conditions which excite comment from a brewer, an ignorant vicar, a lord, and a king. After Conscience has responded briefly to the last of these, the dream breaks up suddenly, with the departure of the vicar:

> The viker hadde fer hoom, and faire took his leeve—
> And I awakned therwith, and wroot as me mette.
>
> (XIX. 484–5)

It is hard to imagine any other medieval poet ending a dream so: 'The vicar had a long way to go home and said goodbye politely.' That line at a single stroke transforms a scene of apocalyptic significance into an episode from the everyday world where guests having furthest to go leave first; and this transformation reflects back upon Conscience and his largely unavailing efforts to shake the people out of their habitual routines. Invited to partake of 'breed yblessed, and Goddes body therunder', the vicar remembers that he 'has far home' and excuses himself.

But what Langland does best is a different kind of abrupt dream-ending, already perfected by earlier poets. Here the dreamer will be woken by some peak of intensity in the dream experience: a loud noise, some other acute physical sensation, or a sudden surge of emotion. Thus, to cite two post-fourteenth-century examples, the dreamer in William Dunbar's *Golden Targe* is woken by the 'crak' of a broadside fired off by a ship in his dream; and in John Skelton's *Bowge of Courte* it is a moment of terror that triggers the waking. After a series of nightmare experiences on the ship of court, Skelton's dreamer is on the point of jumping overboard:

> Me thoughte I see lewde felawes here and there
> Came for to slee me of mortall entente.
> And as they came, the shypborde faste I hente,
> And thoughte to lepe; and even with that woke,
> Caughte penne and ynke, and wroth this lytell boke.[10]

Langland could have learned the trick from Deguileville, all three of whose dreams conclude in this fashion. The Pilgrimage of Human Life ends, inevitably, with death; and it is the stroke of Death's scythe that wakes the dreamer in a sweat, after which he rises and goes to matins.[11] In the *Pelerinage de l'Ame*, the soul's posthumous journey finally brings it into the presence of the archangel Michael. Here the light is so bright that it forces the dreamer to open his eyes, which have been closed in sleep—a particularly subtle variant on this type of ending:

> Une clarte du lieu hautain
> Sus mes yeux descendi a plain
> Et tantost les me fist ouvrir
> Que clos avoie par dormir.
> Eveille fu et me trouvai
> En mon lit.[12]

The third and last of Deguileville's *Pelerinages*, that of Jesus Christ, ends with the heavenly host singing and playing in celebration of Christ's Ascension and the Assumption of the Virgin Mary; and it is this 'chanterie grant' that wakes the poet from his sleep.[13]

Langland employs this kind of ending in five out of his ten dreams. In four of the five, characteristically, it is a surge of distress, confusion, or unsatisfied longing that jolts the dreamer abruptly back into the waking world. The least interesting of these moments is the earliest, where Will is awakened at the end of his dream of the pilgrimage to Truth by the quarrel between Piers and the priest:

---

[10] *The Bowge of Courte*, lines 528–32, ed. John Scattergood, *John Skelton: The Complete English Poems* (Harmondsworth, 1983).

[11] *Le Pelerinage de Vie Humaine de Guillaume de Deguileville*, ed. J. J. Stürzinger, Roxburghe Club (London, 1893), lines 13491–506.

[12] Ed. Stürzinger, lines 11006–11: 'A dazzling light from that high place fell directly upon my eyes and at once made me open them, previously closed in sleep. I woke, and found myself in my bed.'

[13] See further Appendix A here.

> The preest and Perkyn apposeden either oother—
> And I thorugh hir wordes awook, and waited aboute,
> And seigh the sonne in the south sitte that tyme.
>
> (VII. 139–41)

Later, at the end of the first dream-within-a-dream, Will wakes himself up with an access of shame, prompted by Reason's rebuke:

> Tho caughte I colour anoon and comsed to ben ashamed,
> And awaked therwith. Wo was me thanne
> That I in metels ne myghte moore have yknowen.
>
> (XI. 403–5)

It is then pointed out to Will that, if he had been able to restrain the impetuosity which earned Reason's rebuke, he would have dreamed and learned more. One may be reminded here of *Pearl*, where the dreamer's impetuous plunge towards the river separating him from the Heavenly City jerks him out of his dream and cuts short his revelations. In dreams, as Yeats said, begin responsibilities. The dream of Patience, which follows in Passus XIII and Passus XIV, ends just as abruptly, this time with a cry of penitential longing from Hawkin, a man driven to a desperate sense of his own worthlessness by the teachings of Patience:

> 'I were noght worthi, woot God,' quod Haukyn,
>   'to werien any clothes,
> Ne neither sherte ne shoon, save for shame one
> To covere my careyne,' quod he, and cride mercy faste,
> And wepte and wailede—and therwith I awakede.
>
> (XIV. 329–32)

Hawkin's cry for mercy anticipates the equally abrupt end of Will's last dream—the very end of the poem, in fact. As Holy Church appears to be on the point of capitulation to the forces of Antichrist, Conscience resolves to set out in search of Piers the Plowman:

>                          'Now Kynde me avenge,
> And sende me hap and heele, til I have Piers the Plowman!'
> And siththe he gradde after Grace, til I gan awake.
>
> (XX. 385–7)

It would be a romantic misreading to take these cries as hopeless—the grace and mercy of God are, of course, realities for Langland—but the note of frustration which they strike is characteristic of many of the poem's story-ends. Indeed, the only one of the dreams that reaches a fully affirmative conclusion is that of the Harrowing of Hell in Passus XVIII. Here, Christ's conquest of Hell is celebrated in a festival of music. Angels harp and sing, Peace pipes, Truth trumpets, Love lutes, and the Four Daughters of God dance and sing a *carole*. This fortissimo finale was most probably suggested by the 'chanterie grant' which concludes the dream in Deguileville's *Pelerinage de Jhesucrist*;[14] but there is more than dream music to wake Long Will:

Til the day dawed thise damyseles carolden,
That men rongen to the resurexion—and right with that I wakede,
And called Kytte my wif and Calote my doghter:
'Ariseth and reverenceth Goddes resurexion'.

(XVIII. 427–30)

This is the most complex and satisfying of Langland's dream endings, since it involves an imaginative fusion of waking experience and dream. The vision of the Harrowing of Hell has taken place in darkness—the darkness of Hell itself, lit only by the coming of Christ. This is first perceived, thrillingly, as a mysterious light appearing there on the horizon; and the promise of a new day, which that light held out, is now fulfilled: 'Til the day dawed thise damyseles carolden'. It is first and foremost the light of the redemption, of which the prophet Isaiah was held to have spoken: 'The people that walked in darkness have seen a great light' (Isaiah 9: 2). It also carries Langland's narrative of the Passion forward to the dawning of the day of the Resurrection itself; but the Easter bells which ring out in the next line, although they blend with the dream music of the heavenly damsels, turn out to belong to a different world—the world of modern waking reality in which Will, responding to the morning call of his local church, is to rise from bed and attend the Easter mass.

---

[14] See Appendix A.

Langland was by no means the first to conceive that an
event in the waking world might coincide with, and by
implication prompt, one of those peaks in the dreaming
experience which so often jolt the dreamer awake. There is
a near analogue in Deguileville again, this time in his *Pelerinage
de Vie Humaine*. While the dream there ends in the agony of
death, this event coincides, as in Langland's poem, with the
ringing of a church bell in the waking world. Thus, in the
Middle English translation of the poem: 'Þus me thouhte as I
mette, but as I was in swich plyte and in swich torment, I
herde þe orlage of þe couent þat rang for þe Matynes as it
was wont. Whan I herde it I awook, and al swetinge I fond
me, and for my meetinge I was gretliche thouhti and abasht.
Algates up I ros me and to Matines I wente.'[15] However,
Langland improves upon this, for whereas Deguileville's
dream death and real bell have nothing intrinsically in com-
mon, Langland's bell both merges with the clamour of
the dream and also bears just the same significance. Both
celebrate the same event, the redemption of mankind, as
recorded in Scripture and as re-enacted in the liturgy of the
Church.

It will be evident from these examples that Langland was
well acquainted with certain established ways of ending dream
stories; but literary tradition offered him no help with his other
structural problem—how to end dreams without stopping the
poem dead in its tracks. For his dream endings are not poem
endings, hardly even in the case of the very last dream, which
concludes so inconclusively. Ideally, therefore, the final chord
upon which each dream ends should contain some unresolved
or discordant note within it, and so create an expectation of
more to come. Only so might the whole strange centrifugal
poly-narrative hold together.

Langland's first connection is one of his best. The first
dream ends with the victory of Conscience and Reason over
Lady Meed at the king's court, a victory which carries with
it the promise of a new spirit of justice and truth flowing
down through the whole system from the highest court in the

[15] *The Pilgrimage of the Lyfe of the Manhode*, ed. Avril Henry, vol. i, EETS 288 (1985),
lines 7271–6.

land. But the king's enthusiasm for this new deal seems a little easy and thoughtless, and Conscience strikes the warning discordant note:

> Quod Conscience to the Kyng, 'But the commune wole assente,
> It is ful hard, by myn heed, herto to brynge it,
> And alle youre lige leodes to lede thus evene.'
>
> (IV. 182–4)

These words act as the cue or catchword for the following dream, with its story of the pilgrimage to Truth; for that pilgrimage represents the attempt to win the assent of the whole community to the new moral regime, as a necessary condition of the public and administrative reform initiated at Westminster. Only when the people individually conform to the ideals promulgated there by Reason and Conscience, and represented now by Piers the Plowman, can they expect to live in the just society envisaged by their enthusiastic king.

The link between this second dream and what follows is rather less clearly articulated. The quarrel between Piers and the priest, with which it concludes, raises a new issue that is to bulk large later, the question of the place and value of learning in the Christian life; but neither this unresolved issue nor Piers's proleptic speech about his proposed new way of life turns out to provide the cue for the ensuing third dream. That cue is provided by the term 'Dowel'. This term emerges for the first time out of the language of the pardon which Piers receives from Truth in Passus VII: '*qui bona egerunt ibunt in vitam eternam*', 'those who have done good things will go into eternal life'. The priest, representing the conventional educated clergy, can see nothing to get excited about in this simple quotation from the Athanasian Creed; and it does indeed seem something of an anticlimax that the moral ideal so richly adumbrated in the events of the preceding dreams should prove capable of being so baldly summarized. But Long Will is excited rather than disappointed. Waking from his dream, he reflects on what he now for the first time calls Dowel; and it is in search of knowledge of this Dowel that he sets off in the fresh dream. What has been seen, albeit imperfectly realized, in the vision of the pilgrimage to Truth

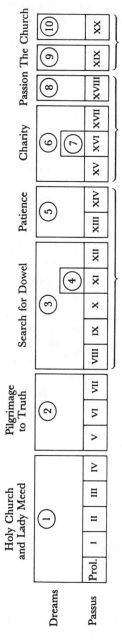

The Ten Dreams of the B Text.

is now to be tracked down and mastered intellectually—or so Will supposes.

Structurally and thematically considered, the remaining eight dreams (constituting the so-called *Vita* section) fall into three distinguishable sequences, of three, three, and two dreams respectively, represented by bracketing here in the diagram on p.19. The two three-dream sequences, which between them carry the poem from Passus VIII to Passus XVIII, exhibit a rather remarkable similarity in their organ-ization. In each, the second of the dreams is contained within the first, as a dream-within-a-dream; and in each that inner dream looks forward to, and is completed by, the third, concluding dream.[16]

The first sequence extends from Passus VIII to Passus XIV inclusive. Its three dreams concern, respectively, the search for Dowel (VIII–XII), the chastening of Long Will (the inner dream, XI), and Patience (XIII–XIV). These sections exhibit both the strengths and the weaknesses of Langland's fictive imagination; but for the moment I am concerned only with their relations one to another. These depend, though with many digressions on the way, upon two governing preoccupa-tions. From the start, Will is concerned to discover the meaning of Dowel and its offshoots, Dobet and Dobest; and his prolonged enquiry does arrive at a kind of conclusion at the end of the first dream in the sequence, when in Passus XII Imaginatif resolves some of his difficulties and concludes by reaffirming the message of Truth's pardon.[17] But by this

---

[16] It will be observed that these three 'sequences' correspond to the three sections 'Dowel', 'Dobet', and 'Dobest' distinguished by the rubrics in certain manuscripts of the B Text (Hm, L, and W) and thence in Skeat's edition of the poem. This is 'Type 1' among the several 'segmentation patterns' analysed by Robert Adams in his article, 'The Reliability of the Rubrics in the B-Text of *Piers Plowman*', *Medium Aevum*, 54 (1985), 208–31. Adams regards these rubrics as 'the wrong-headed offspring of some mediaeval editor' (p. 209); but even he observes a certain structural felicity in the divisions they mark: 'an early editor of a B-version manuscript conveniently matched the terminology of the *Do*-triad to pairs of the poem's outer dreams [not counting, that is, the dreams-within-dreams] so as to produce the tetradic structure implied by the rubrics' (p. 214 n. 7). It is not clear to me why Adams regards variation between the manuscripts in their segmentation patterns as evidence that no authorial pattern lies behind them. Why should such a pattern not have been subject, like the authorial text, to scribal interference?

[17] B XII. 285–92. The connection between Passus XII and the dream which it resumes, after the interruption by the inner dream in XI, is marked by the only clear

time, Will's intellectual difficulties have come to be seen in a somewhat different light. The dream had begun with a series of encounters, with Thought, Wit, and the rest, in which Will listened more or less docilely to a great deal of rambling talk about Dowel; but in Passus X he suddenly cuts loose, with a fierce tirade in which he casts doubt on the fundamental assumption that God does indeed reward those who do well, as Truth's pardon promised. God's system of rewards, he protests, so far from seeming just and reasonable, appears to pay scant regard to human effort or human merit. Virtue and intelligence, he objects, are *not* always rewarded with eternal life, for is not Aristotle among the damned? Nor are stupidity and vice always punished, for did not Christ promise salvation to the thief on the cross? So, what price Dowel?

One's sense of this as a real crisis in the argument of the poem is confirmed by the fact that the A Text broke off, with its dream unfinished, at just this point, and also, perhaps, by the fact that, when the poet returned to continue where he had left off, he resorted first to an unprecedented device: the dream-within-a-dream, in Passus XI of the B Text. That inner dream offers a first response to the soteriological objections raised by Will in his tirade, by confronting him, weirdly, with the figure of the Roman Emperor Trajan. Trajan is represented as a pagan who has none the less achieved salvation by virtue of his good life. So Dowel does indeed save: '*qui bona egerunt ibunt in vitam eternam*'. But the prime effect of this strange dream is, I think, to shift the main issue on to a moral, even a personal, plane. Will is not so much answered as chastened, and the dream ends, not in intellectual assent, but in an access of shame. It has confronted Will with his own faults and invited him to learn through self-knowledge the wisdom of 'suffraunce' or patience. So, when he wakes back into his original dream, he tells Imaginatif that he knows now what Dowel is: ' "To se muche and suffre moore, certes," quod I,

case of narrative prolepsis in the B Text. At X. 117, Dame Study promises Will that 'Ymaginatif herafterward shal answer to youre purpos'—which Imaginatif duly does, in his fashion, in XII. On narrative prolepsis, see Gérard Genette, *Narrative Discourse*, trans. J. E. Lewin (Oxford, 1980). A valuable discussion of Passus IX–XII, and especially of the inner dream there, is by Joseph S. Wittig, '*Piers Plowman* B, Passus IX–XII: Elements in the Design of the Inward Journey', *Traditio*, 28 (1972), 211–80.

"is Dowel" ' (XI. 410). This new preoccupation with 'suf-
fraunce' based upon knowledge of self looks forward, beyond
the ensuing scene with Imaginatif which concludes the old
dream, to the new dream of Passus XIII–XIV—one domi-
nated by Patience himself, in person. The former preoccupa-
tions with Dowel and its intellectual difficulties are not to be
immediately set aside; but it seems to matter little now that
Imaginatif's treatment of these problems should have ap-
peared, as it did, somewhat sketchy. The poem's focus of
attention has moved on. Indeed, when the new dream opens
with the dinner at Conscience's house, discussion of Dowel
has become a matter of high-table conversation in which Will
participates, so far as he participates at all, from some distance
away in the body of the hall, where he sits with his humble
dinner-companion, Patience. And when, at the end of this
scene, Conscience leaves his own dinner party to set out on
pilgrimage with Patience and encounter Hawkin, the trans-
ition from Dowel to Patience, and such moral progression as
that implies, is complete.

Hawkin's near-despairing cry for mercy, with which the
Dowel/Patience sequence ends, evokes its response in the
following sequence of three dreams, culminating in the vision
of the Redemption in Passus XVIII. The thematic unity of
this sequence is very clear. Its subject is charity: described by
Anima in Passus XV, emblematically represented in the Tree
of Charity in XVI, and exemplified in the ensuing version of
the life of Christ.[18] Structurally it is less satisfactory, as if
repeating somewhat mechanically the pattern of the preceding
sequence. In particular, the inner dream here disrupts the
fictional integrity of the dream within which it is set, as the
earlier one did not. There, the first dream had been convin-
cingly resumed with the figure of Imaginatif, who recognizably
belongs with Thought, Wit, Study, and the rest. But here,
when Will wakes from his inner dream, he encounters first
Faith, then Hope and Charity, and the action, though it
moves powerfully towards the climax of the Passion, has
nothing to establish its narrative continuity with the earlier

---

[18] The thematic transition from patience to charity is marked by B XVI. 8–9:
'Pacience hatte the pure tree, and pore symple of herte, | And so thorugh God and
thorugh goode men groweth the fruyt Charite.'

part of the same dream, in which Will had met Anima.[19] So this, for once, is a broken-backed dream. Certainly the build-up to the climax of the sequence is very powerfully done: the version of Christ's life which concludes the inner dream breaks off in the darkness of Maundy Thursday, with Jesus taken into captivity by night, and the ensuing vision of Faith, Hope, and Charity streaming towards Jerusalem for the great event sustains the sense of rising excitement already created by the inner dream. But there is something a little awkward in our finding ourselves, as Passus XVIII opens, back at Palm Sunday, having already reached the following Thursday at the end of the inner dream.

None the less, the Palm Sunday opening of the last dream of this sequence makes brilliant use of the imaginative possibilities of a discontinuous dream fiction:

> Oon semblable to the Samaritan, and somdeel to
>   Piers the Plowman,
> Barefoot on an asse bak bootles cam prikye,
> Withouten spores other spere; spakliche he loked,
> As is the kynde of a knyght that cometh to be dubbed,
> To geten hym gilte spores on galoches ycouped.
>                                   (XVIII. 10–14)

There may always be, as has been observed, a question of identity as between one dream and another in *Piers Plowman*: Conscience is the same person wherever he appears, but the Peace of XVIII is not the same as the Peace of IV. Here the relationship is more complex, however. In the preceding inner dream, Piers has just made his first appearance (first in the B Text) since the pardon scene; and when Will woke back into his outer dream, it was for Piers that he looked, in vain:

> And I awaked therwith, and wiped myne eighen,
> And after Piers the Plowman pried and stared.
>                                   (XVI. 167–8)

[19] In the C Text, XVIII. 179–81, Langland attempted to strengthen the unity of the dream by introducing a reference back to Liberum Arbitrium—the C-Text substitute for B's Anima—at the moment of awakening: 'With moche noyse þat nyhte nere frentyk y wakede; | In inwit and in alle wittes aftur *Liberum Arbitrium* | Y waytede witterly, ac whoder he wende y ne wiste.' He had, however, already weakened the structure of the dream by omitting the lines in B (XVI. 18–20) which describe Will's falling asleep into his inner dream; so, in C, this inner dream has a stronger ending but no beginning.

But he finds something like the satisfaction he seeks in the figure of the Good Samaritan. I referred earlier to the three figures who dominate the resumed outer dream as Faith, Hope, and Charity; but their identities are in fact more questionable than that. Indeed, the last and greatest of them, to whom Will attaches himself, is never called Charity at all. He is the Samaritan of Christ's parable. Yet, unlike the figure in the parable, he is riding towards Jerusalem on a mule; and that suggests for him a further, historical, identity—the Christ of the Entry into Jerusalem. Furthermore, it is not simply the Samaritan who rides in at the beginning of the next dream on an ass's back, but 'someone looking like the Samaritan and rather like Piers the Plowman'. The two heroes of the previous dream thus seem to blend into a new, composite hero, very much in dream fashion. Langland was fond of introducing new characters without at first identifying them; but here the 'oon' ('someone') formula has a special felicity. Jesus, in the poet's version, rides into Jerusalem as a knight coming to the joust. He reminds Will of the Samaritan partly because what he last dreamed was the Samaritan riding off 'like the wind' towards Jerusalem, and partly because the ass recalls the Samaritan's mule; and he brings Piers to mind because, as we learn later, he is wearing his armour. But fourteenth-century armour hid the identity of its wearer from all except those equipped to identify a coat-of-arms on shield or coat; and it is therefore left for Faith, who is a herald of arms, to name the jouster for Will's benefit as Jesus, son of David. So what was foreshadowed in parable and fantasy in the previous dream here becomes a reality—albeit a reality still swaddled in the mystery of dream, which is here also the mystery of incarnation.

By the beginning of Passus XVIII, the poem has conformed itself to the order of historical time, and it is that order which determines the relationships of the remaining dreams. Thus, the penultimate dream (Passus XIX) opens with a vision of the Christ of the Resurrection, narrates the coming of the Holy Spirit at Pentecost and the founding of the apostolic Church under Piers (here identified with St Peter), and ends with a contrasting vision of the modern Church under attack from Pride and his followers. In the last dream, the subject

is again the Church in Langland's own day, on the point of
capitulation to the forces of an Antichrist. Structurally con-
sidered, the poem's last three dreams, each of which occupies
a single passus, resemble rather too much the conventional
chapters or 'books' of a narrative text. Thus, the break before
Passus XVIII might be compared to the break between Books
II and III in Chaucer's *Troilus*: in both, the reader is left in
suspense, awaiting what is evidently to be a great moment in
the story. Similarly, the next dream division does little more
than punctuate the fantastic historical narrative at the conclu-
sion of the climactic Harrowing of Hell. And for the division
between the last two dreams I can see no good justification
at all, unless it was to make space for the strange waking
interlude between Will and Need. The vision of the tottering
contemporary Church seems to be interrupted quite arbitrarily
when the vicar makes his apologies at the end of Passus
XIX—good as that moment is in itself—and the next dream
simply resumes the same subject. Admittedly, the last dream
opens with a coming of Antichrist; but that momentous event
appears to make little difference to a situation already suffi-
ciently desperate. It is as if the dividing off of dreams had
become for the poet, at last, a somewhat mechanical process.

   There is nothing mechanical, however, about the way the
last dream ends, and with it the poem:

   'By Crist!' quod Conscience tho, 'I wole bicome a pilgrym,
   And walken as wide as the world lasteth,
   To seken Piers the Plowman, that Pryde myghte destruye,
   And that freres hadde a fyndyng, that for nede flateren
   And countrepledeth me, Conscience. Now Kynde me avenge,
   And sende me hap and heele, til I have Piers the Plowman!'
   And siththe he gradde after Grace, til I gan awake.

                                          (XX. 381–7)

Unlike the ending of the *Roman de la Rose*, quoted earlier, this
abrupt ending does not seem merely cursory or impatient.
One reason for this is that the sequence of historically ordered
dreams in the latter part of Langland's poem has brought him
to the point where there is nothing left but the future. If he
were a prophetic writer like Joachim of Flora, that future
might itself furnish matter for visionary description; but,

despite the appearance of an Antichrist, Conscience does not speak as if the end of the world were nigh. As A. C. Spearing points out, his curiously expressed resolution to 'walken as wide as the world lasteth' implies extension in time as well as in space.[20] There is indeed to be a future, but that future can be the subject only of resolutions, longings, and prayer. Conscience can imagine solutions to the present plight of the Church, with the hoped-for help of Piers, Nature, and Grace; and Langland even finds room to mention one specific remedy—the regular endowment of the friars, so that they may no longer depend upon begging. But such velleities are not the stuff of which future visions are made. The poem has come to the end of the line.

Yet *Piers Plowman* as a complete whole can hardly be imagined in this way—as following a 'line' of historical time up to the point where it comes to a stop in the present. On the contrary, indeed, it is commonly taken by readers to form some kind of circle. The immediate source of this impression is clear enough. Though the historically ordered sequence of dreams begins in the past, in Passus XVI, with a sudden plunge into Old Testament times, the poem as a whole begins in the present, with the dreams of Lady Meed and of the pilgrimage to Truth. So the movement from the apostolic Church to its unmiraculous modern successor, which takes place in Passus XIX, in fact has the effect of returning the reader to the world in which the poem began. Also, the re-establishment there of Piers in his original role of ploughman (albeit now of a highly metaphorical kind) brings with it a return to something like the agricultural world of the half acre in Passus VI. Yet there is also a deeper sense of circularity, which arises not from the presence of the Plowman in Passus XIX but from his absence at the poem's end. The Piers of XIX, identified with the St Peter of the Gospels and Acts, represented the Church in its full charismatic strength; but at some point which Langland does not attempt to locate historically that strength has left the Church. So Piers is now mysteriously elsewhere, and to find him Conscience has to

---

[20] *Medieval Dream-Poetry* (Cambridge, 1976), 159. It should be noted, however, that George Kane and E. T. Donaldson, in their edition of the B Text (London, 1975), reject *lasteth* as scribal and substitute *renneþ* from C.

search 'as wide as the world lasteth'. This is an ending which could just as well be a beginning—a beginning set in the confused and Piersless world of the Prologue. It is as if, as in Joyce's *Finnegans Wake*, the ideal reader suffering from ideal insomnia were invited to go straight back and start reading the poem over again.

This is one aspect of what might be called the unprogressive nature of *Piers Plowman*. In this poem, as one critic puts it, 'nothing that does happen seems very much to affect anything else that happens'.[21] It is as if the normal rules of consequentiality do not apply. The dreamer can be told over and over again what Dowel is without ever knowing the answer; and even Christ's sacrifice may seem to have had little effect, to judge by the present state of things as portrayed in the two last passus. Further, the ten dreams are unprogressive on the thematic as well as on the narrative level. One can indeed see the series as passing gradually from one spiritual theme to another. The theme of 'truth' in the first two dreams gives way to that of 'Dowel', which is in turn replaced by 'patience'; and patience, to use the poet's own metaphor, bears the fruit 'charity'; and the key term in the last two dreams is 'unity'. But the rolling sequence truth–Dowel–patience–charity–unity is not, in the event, a progressive sequence. One might say, rather, that each term points inwards, towards a single spiritual centre whose position is suggested, as the poem's title implies, by the figure of Piers the Plowman.

---

[21] Mary Carruthers, 'Time, Apocalypse, and the Plot of *Piers Plowman*', in M. J. Carruthers and E. D. Kirk (eds.), *Acts of Interpretation: The Text in its Contexts 700–1600. Essays on Medieval and Renaissance Literature in Honor of E. Talbot Donaldson* (Norman, Okla., 1982), 175–88; 176. See also Anne Middleton, 'Narration and the Invention of Experience: Episodic Form in *Piers Plowman*', in L. D. Benson and S. Wenzel (eds.), *The Wisdom of Poetry: Essays in Early English Literature in Honor of Morton W. Bloomfield* (Kalamazoo, Mich., 1982), 91–122. Middleton describes the arrangement of Langland's episodes as 'somehow reiterative rather than progressive' (p. 92).

CHAPTER 2

# Fictions of the Divided Mind

After Long Will has woken from the second of his dreams, he is left musing on the significance of what he has seen, and also on the meaning of dreams in general. He has been impressed by his vision of Piers the Plowman; but—

> Ac I have no savour in songewarie, for I se it ofte faille;
> Caton and canonistres counseillen us to leve
> To sette sadnesse in songewarie—for *sompnia ne cures.*
> Ac for the book Bible bereth witnesse
> How Daniel divined the dremes of a kyng...
>
> (VII. 149–53)

And so on. Langland is not the only dream poet to marshal arguments for and against 'songewarie' or dream interpretation;[1] but the lines here quoted are highly characteristic of him in the movement of their thought, and especially in their use of the strong adversative conjunction *ac*, 'but', 'on the other hand'. Will's dream has been remarkable, but *(ac)* he has no taste for dream interpretation. The school author Cato and experts in canon law advise us not to look for serious meaning in dreams, *ac* the Bible on the other hand reports undoubted cases where they have foretold the future.

Langland's *ac*s are a recurrent sign and expression of what in this chapter I shall call—using the expression somewhat loosely—his 'divided mind'. There are, of course, matters upon which Langland's mind was, on the evidence of the poem, far from divided: one may even remember him chiefly as a poet of passionate convictions—by contrast, perhaps, with Geoffrey Chaucer. Yet it is also true that few poets, and certainly few medieval poets, convey such a strong sense of the sheer difficulty of making up one's mind on certain issues—whether or not in the end one succeeds in doing so.

---

[1] e.g. *Le Roman de la Rose*, ed. Lecoy, lines 1–10, with a 'but' *(mes)* at line 3. On medieval thinking about 'songewarie', for and against, see Steven F. Kruger, *Dreaming in the Middle Ages* (Cambridge, 1992).

How can God be, as he certainly is, both entirely just and entirely merciful at once? What is the proper response to requests made by beggars? Can the life of a merchant or a minstrel be morally justified? Do pardons have any value? These are some of the questions to which, as readers of the poem will recall, Langland finds no easy answers—if indeed he finds any answer at all. It may be that the authorities differ among themselves, as in the case of dreams; or one's own experience may be confused and confusing; or reason itself may prompt conflicting arguments in the mind, *pro* and *contra*, *sic* and *non*.

The mind has its own ways of dealing with such conflicts. One way is to look for distinctions, as the scholastic philosopher did with his *distinguo*. Langland has some knowledge of this scholastic method, and he employs it on occasion, most notably when Conscience attempts to cut through the fog of confusion surrounding Lady Meed by distinguishing 'two manere of medes' (III. 231). But the poet's distinctions are commonly of a less formal and technical kind, as when he tries, not without difficulty, to sort out his mixed feelings about minstrels by dividing them into good and bad ones—a process of thought that continues and develops through all three versions of the poem, as E. T. Donaldson has shown.[2] Here, however, I shall be concerned with a more specifically poetic way of handling such contentious issues, through the creation of fictions—fictions of the divided mind. What is achieved in such fictions is not the kind of intellectually satisfying solution that Aquinas aimed at in his handling of *pro* and *contra* arguments in the *Summa Theologica*. Rather, in the poem Langland projects his conflicting thoughts and feelings into a dream narrative, an imaginary world where conflict may perhaps be set at rest. This is one of the uses of fiction.

The literary traditions available to Langland offered him one sort of narrative specifically adapted to the expression of conflicting thoughts. This was the debate, or *conflictus*, imagined as taking place between spokesmen of rival positions.[3]

[2] *Piers Plowman: The C-Text and its Poet* (New Haven, Conn., 1949), 136–55.
[3] See generally Thomas L. Reed, *Middle English Debate Poetry and the Aesthetics of Irresolution* (Columbia, Mo., 1990).

Most relevant here is what has been called the 'horizontal' debate, where the disputants appear to be on an equal footing in their competition for readers' sympathy or assent. This is to be distinguished from the other type of debate, less happily known as 'vertical', where one participant does little more than feed questions and objections to a superior authority, as Boethius does to Lady Philosophy in the *Consolatio Philosophiae*, or the dreamer to the pearl maiden in *Pearl*. This latter type is fully represented in *Piers Plowman*, in Will's encounters with such authorities as Lady Holy Church; but it is perhaps surprising that Langland makes so little use of the horizontal type. One might have expected that its potentially more problematical character would have appealed to him. There was a fine English model in a poem of the 1350s, *Winner and Waster*, which sets out opposing views, on what in a later age would be called the use of riches, in the form of a debate between the two personifications named in its title.

It may be that such formal, horizontal debating smelt a little too much of the schools for Langland's taste. However that may be, there is only one clear example in the whole poem, and that of a quite conventional kind: the debate of the Four Daughters of God in Passus XVIII. This narrative has its roots in a passage in one of the Psalms: 'Surely his salvation is near to them that fear him: that glory may dwell in our land. Mercy and truth have met each other: justice and peace have kissed' (Psalm 84: 11–12, AV 85: 9–10). From these verses, taken in conjunction with a reference to God's 'daughters' in Isaiah 43: 6, the rabbinic and Christian imagination constructed a scene in which Misericordia, Veritas, Justitia, and Pax are personified as young women meeting and embracing.[4] The scene is most commonly set as a kind of prologue to the incarnation of Christ, as in Deguileville's *Pelerinage de Jhesucrist*, or sometimes as part of the judgement of an individual after death, as in Deguileville's *Pelerinage de l'Ame* or the English moral play *The Castle of Perseverance*.[5]

[4] See Hope Traver, *The Four Daughters of God* (Philadelphia, 1907), and Kari Sajavaara (ed.), *The Middle English Translations of Robert Grosseteste's 'Chateau d'Amour'*, Mémoires de la Société Néophilologique de Helsinki, 32 (1967), 62–90.

[5] *Le Pelerinage Jhesucrist de Guillaume de Deguileville*, ed. J. J. Stürzinger, Roxburghe Club (London, 1897), lines 297–664; *Pelerinage de l'Ame*, ed. Stürzinger, lines 1075–2556;

Langland is apparently the only author to place the scene, as he most effectively does, in Hell—at the moment when a strange light first announces the approach of the crucified Christ, descending into the darkness for the Harrowing of Hell. This is a notable example of the way in which scriptural passages could stimulate Langland's imagination to create pictures and scenes. The imminence of Christ was suggested by the first part of the passage from Psalms: 'Surely his salvation is near to them that fear him'; and the following words, 'that glory may dwell in our land', must have further suggested the marvellous chiaroscuro of the setting, with the darkness of Hell first touched by a dawning light, and also the point of view from which it is seen. For King David, the supposed author of the Psalm, was one of those for whom Hell was destined to be 'our land' until the moment of the Harrowing; and the word *gloria*, itself strongly suggestive of light in Christian usage, would have reminded the poet of that other Psalm where the Christ of the Harrowing is prophetically spoken of as the 'King of glory' who is to throw open the gates of Hell and enter in (Psalm 23, AV 24). So it is as if Langland, pondering this passage from the book of the Bible he knew best, and conceiving it in a concrete and dramatic fashion, found his new setting for the Four Daughters of God ready made for him there.

The two conflicting issues here are justice and mercy. Where human agents are concerned, these two principles present a mainly practical problem of judgement—the problem of tempering justice with mercy. This was seen as an undoubted obligation upon kings, lords, judges, and the like; but the difficulty is to decide quite how merciful to be, and on what occasion. In the case of God, however, the problem is somewhat different. God is generally understood to be at all times both absolutely just and absolutely merciful; but it is hard for human minds to see how to reconcile these two dogmatic truths. This difficulty comes to a head in Langland's poem in Passus XVIII, with his treatment of the Harrowing

*The Castle of Perseverance*, ed. Mark Eccles, *The Macro Plays*, EETS 262 (1969), lines 3129–597. Deguileville, in both *Jhesucrist* and *Ame*, has only three daughters: Justice, Verité, and Misericorde.

of Hell. Considered in the context of the whole history of
mankind as recorded in the Bible, the salvation which Christ
brought is quite evidently an act of mercy; but how can it
also be considered just? This question haunts the Harrowing
sequence throughout. When Mercy and Truth first meet in
the darkness they argue about it, as do their sisters Peace and
Righteousness later. Then Satan and Lucifer take the matter
up, from their own different point of view. And finally Christ
adds his voice, in the great speech which he makes as he
gathers 'them that fear him' into his light.

Langland characteristically develops both sides of the argu-
ment quite fully, *pro* and *contra*. Truth, who here represents
fidelity to principle, is the first to object that God's redemption
of man cannot be reconciled with his justice. She cites the
authority of Job, who stated that 'there can be no release from
Hell'.[6] Righteousness supports her, recalling that Adam and
Eve and their descendants were all condemned by the Fall to
death and eternal punishment, 'Forthi lat hem chewe as thei
chosen' (XVIII. 200). Lucifer, in his turn, invokes the same
judgement, and objects that, if God now deprived the devils
of what is theirs by right, he will be acting against reason,
right, and law—using mere *force majeure*, in fact: 'If he reve
me of my right, he robbeth me by maistrie' (276). Langland
clearly felt the full force of this argument: God is bound to
act justly, even in his dealings with devils.[7] Hence the counter-
arguments all have to try to show, as if in a court of law, that
the Redemption is indeed right and reasonable. The main
lines of defence, employed by Mercy and later by Christ
himself, find expression in a series of rhetorical parallels: the
tree of knowledge and the tree of the Cross, Christ's life for
man's, death for death, soul for soul, and so on. The most
remarkable of these arguments is put forward by Christ:

---

[6] XVIII. 149a. Job 7: 9 is similar, but the exact words used by Truth occur rather
in the Office of the Dead, as well as in penitential handbooks: see N. Gray, *Modern
Philology*, 84 (1986–7), 58.

[7] Myra Stokes, *Justice and Mercy in Piers Plowman: A Reading of the B Text Visio* (London,
1984), 268: 'the most striking aspect of Langland's account of the Crucifixion and
Harrowing is the way in which these events, traditionally associated so centrally with
the mercy of God, are represented consistently and insistently as a triumph for and
a vindication of His justice'.

'Thow, Lucifer, in liknesse of a luther addere
Getest bi gile tho that God lovede;
And I, in liknesse of a leode, that Lord am of hevene,
Graciousliche thi gile have quyt—go gile ayein gile!'
(XVIII. 355–8)

Guile against guile! Lucifer took a step down in the order of created beings from fallen angel to adder when he deceived Eve; so Christ can fairly do the same trick, stepping down from godhead to manhood, when he sets out to repair the damage.

The sublime music of the speech imagined by Langland for Christ carries all before it—it is one of the high points of the poem.[8] Yet one may question just how seriously the actual arguments are meant. They are not merely rhetorical, yet they surely fall short, in their witty luxuriance, of strict demonstration.[9] So it is not inappropriate that the difficulties should be set finally to rest not by argument but by poetic fiction. Earlier the Four Daughters had 'met together'; now, as the Psalmist also prophesied, they kiss, and the dream ends in their *carole*: 'Til the day dawed thise damyseles carolden' (427). Langland uses the word *carole* here in its earliest English sense, 'a ring-dance in which the dancers themselves sing the governing music'.[10] So the Psalmist's symbolic kiss is here reinforced by other symbols of harmonious unity: joining hands, dancing, and singing together. This is a case of a real intellectual difficulty, arising from the demands of two apparently incompatible dogmatic truths, being resolved by symbolic action. Perhaps the effect is a little too easily achieved; but it is clearly

[8] The Langlandian sublime was recognized in the eighteenth century: Thomas Warton, *The History of English Poetry*, rev. edn., 4 vols. (London, 1824), ii. 119–20, citing B XX. 80–109.

[9] See, however, Anna P. Baldwin, 'The Double Duel in *Piers Plowman* B XVIII and C XXI', *Medium Aevum*, 50 (1981), 64–78, arguing that Christ establishes an indisputable right to possess mankind and condemn Lucifer by virtue of two legal processes, civil duel of law and duel of chivalry. See also William J. Birnes, 'Christ as Advocate: The Legal Metaphor of *Piers Plowman*', *Annuale Mediaevale*, 16 (1975), 71–93, and John A. Alford, 'Literature and Law in Medieval England', *PMLA* 92 (1977), 941–51. Legalisms in the language can be traced in Alford, *Piers Plowman: A Glossary of Legal Diction* (Cambridge, 1988).

[10] Richard Leighton Greene, *The Early English Carols*, 2nd edn. (Oxford, 1977), p. xxiii.

preferable to the kind of expository solution with which, in
*The Castle of Perseverance*, God brings the dispute of the Daugh-
ters to an end. It sounds like a cook's recipe:

> To make my blysse perfyth
> I menge wyth my most myth
> Alle pes, sum treuthe, and sum ryth,
> And most of my mercy.[11]

Turning back now to the earlier part of the poem, we find
more complex and troubled relationships between fiction and
thought. This is certainly the case in the story of Lady Meed
and her marriage in Passus II–IV. In the episode of the Four
Daughters of God, Langland was handling a well-articulated,
though intractable, intellectual problem, with the help of a
story which was itself already well established as a kind of
imaginary solution to the problem. The story of Lady Meed,
on the other hand, is the poet's own invention, and the
problems with which it deals were less clearly defined. These
are best considered, in fact, as arising directly from the
multiple and unregulated significations of the vernacular word
'mede' itself, as that word was commonly used in Langland's
English. For, unlike most of the words which enter into
his stories as personifications—'mercy', say, or 'reason', or
'wrong'—the word 'mede' had both good and bad meanings
at the time. The customary editorial gloss 'reward' does little
justice to its semantic range in Middle English.[12] The word
commonly referred to the rewards dispensed by God in the
afterlife: 'The day of dome shal come, wer every man shal
han his mede aftyr his desert.'[13] On the other hand, it could
also denote bribes and other immoral gifts, or bribery and
corruption generally, as in Chaucer's reference to 'Genylon-

---

[11] Ed. Eccles, lines 3570–3. Vague quantifications such as this provide only weak
resolutions for the kinds of dilemma considered here. Thus, at B XII. 210–13,
Imaginatif attempts to justify God's decisions in assigning Trajan to Hell and the
penitent thief to Heaven by arguing that the thief was placed lowest in Heaven and
Trajan high in Hell. Placing Trajan 'noght depe in helle' offers a naïve way of
vindicating divine judgements.

[12] See the discussion of the word in David Burnley, *A Guide to Chaucer's Language*
(London, 1983), 203–13. The bearing of its various meanings upon Langland's
allegorical story is best analysed by Myra Stokes, *Justice and Mercy*, ch. 3.

[13] *MED mede* n. (4), sense 2(a). The quotation is from Mandeville.

Olyver, corrupt for meede'.[14] Yet it also, though less commonly, denoted legitimate compensation for services rendered, hence wages or earnings.[15] So the word had three main semantic focuses: divine reward, bribery, and earnings. It is not hard to see that there is likely to be trouble when such a protean word enters a story as a person; and trouble there certainly is in this part of Langland's poem. It might perhaps have been avoided if the poet had attempted to create in Lady Meed a person as complex and morally contradictory as the word itself, or else if he had settled for just one of its various significations and excluded the others altogether from the story. In the event he does neither of these things, and the result is a fiction which has fascinated and confused many readers—and indeed, to judge by the revisions in the B and C Texts, Langland himself. To simplify a complex matter somewhat, I confine the present discussion to three key moments in the story.

The first of these moments is the introduction of Lady Meed into the dream. In ways which a modern reader may not fully appreciate, this introduction firmly establishes her as a thoroughly wicked character, representing 'mede' in its worst possible sense. After hearing about the values of 'truth' from Lady Holy Church in Passus I, Long Will has asked his instructress to teach him to 'knowe the false', truth's opposite. Look to your left, she says, and—

> I loked on my left half as the lady me taughte,
> And was war of a womman wonderliche yclothed—
> Purfiled with pelure, the pureste on erthe,
> Ycorouned with a coroune, the kyng hath noon bettre.
> Fetisliche hire fyngres were fretted with gold wyr,
> And thereon rede rubies as rede as any gleede,

---

[14] *MED* sense 1a (c). I quote 'Monk's Tale', *Canterbury Tales*, VII. 2389.

[15] *MED* sense 1a (b). It may be noted here that the word does not in any of its senses single out money, as against non-pecuniary forms of reward. Lady Meed naturally does on occasion deal in money; but she also deals in 'presents withouten pens' (III. 89) such as bowls, cups, jewels, coats, and even loads of wheat (III. 22–3, 40, 143). I therefore do not agree with David Aers when he argues that Langland is concerned specifically with the bad effects of a developing money economy: *Chaucer, Langland and the Creative Imagination* (London, 1980), 7; also p. 45: 'the forces of Meed represented developments whereby money, economy and market relations were becoming powerful enough to dissolve traditional personal and ethical ties'.

> And diamaundes of derrest pris and double manere saphires,
> Orientals and ewages envenymes to destroye.
> Hire robe was ful riche, of reed scarlet engreyned,
> With ribanes of reed gold and of riche stones.

>                                                (II. 7–16)

Although Will professes himself 'ravished' by what he sees, there is in fact much here to confirm expectations set up by what has gone before—the promise that he will see 'the false', and the command to look to his left, or sinister, side. For this woman is plainly a dream version of the biblical Scarlet Woman or Great Whore of Babylon, described in Apocalypse as a woman 'clothed round about with purple and scarlet, and gilt with gold and precious stones and pearls'.[16] Furthermore, just as St John set the Scarlet Woman in opposition to another lady, the Bride of the Lamb, clad in 'fine linen glittering and white', so Langland contrasts Lady Meed with a 'lovely lady of leere in lynnen yclothed', Lady Holy Church (I. 3). The opposition is as vivid and uncompromising as that between Una and Duessa, derived from the same biblical source, in Spenser's *Faerie Queene*. Like Spenser's Duessa, Lady Meed is evidently to stand for deceit and corruption, as an enemy of the one true bride of the Lamb, the Church. Lady Holy Church herself simply confirms this judgement in what she goes on to tell Will about Meed—that she is a bastard daughter of False, that she takes after her father, and so on.[17]

There is no sign of a divided mind here, nor in the ensuing preparations for Meed's marriage to False. Evil marriages of this sort are among the stock-in-trade of allegorical narrative, and the significance of the present one is unequivocal enough.[18] To give meed to false (without capital letters) is to give bribes to the corrupt. It comes therefore as a considerable

---

[16] Apoc. (Rev.) 17: 4. Lady Meed is later called a whore (IV. 166, and cf. III. 131–3). On the biblical background to this passage, see D. W. Robertson, Jr., and B. F. Huppé, *Piers Plowman and Scriptural Tradition* (Princeton, NJ, 1951), 50–2.

[17] The condemnation by Holy Church becomes progressively more specific, from A II. 16–32 through B II. 20–51 to C II. 19–52.

[18] Compare the motif of the Daughters of the Devil, each of whom marries into an appropriate class of human society. See G. R. Owst, *Literature and Pulpit in Medieval England*, 2nd edn. (Oxford, 1961), 93–6; and, for an Anglo-Norman example, *Le Mariage des neuf filles du diable*, ed. P. Meyer, *Romania*, 29 (1900), 54–72.

surprise that a new character, Theology, should intervene to propose a different, virtuous marriage—for the Scarlet Woman, of all people. Addressing the corrupt lawyers who have connived at the affair, Theology protests that Meed should not marry False. She is a legitimate daughter of Amends, he says; and God has promised her in marriage to truth:

> 'For Mede is muliere, of Amendes engendred;
> And God graunted to gyve Mede to truthe,
> And thow hast gyven hire to a gilour . . .'
>
> (II. 119–21)

There is, it seems to me, no good way of making sense of this intervention on the literal level of the story. In his last revision of the poem, Langland cleared up the question of Meed's parentage by describing Amends as her mother, married to an evil husband (C II. 120–2); but there remains the conflict between Theology's claim that she is legitimate and Holy Church's earlier condemnation of her as a bastard. One might dismiss this objection as pedantic, and take the double parentage as pointing to a double nature in Meed: thus one critic has spoken of her as an 'almost morally neutral' character.[19] But the story simply does not allow this. It is true that Meed plays a passive part in the marriage negotiations. She is just as ready later in the story to marry Conscience as she was to marry False. Yet there can surely be no question of unprejudiced judgement here. Meed is a Scarlet Woman— that has been clearly established at the start—and her compliant behaviour, if it is to be understood novelistically at all, can only be seen as the sinister and self-serving docility of a Becky Sharpe. So how is Theology's intervention to be taken? The key is to understand what he means by saying that 'God has granted to give Meed to truth'. Since the speaker is Theology, the statement must be taken theologically. So taken, it can only refer to 'mede' in its good sense of heavenly reward: God has promised that reward to those who live a

---

[19] A. G. Mitchell, 'Lady Meed and the Art of *Piers Plowman*', in R. J. Blanch (ed.), *Style and Symbolism in 'Piers Plowman': A Modern Critical Anthology* (Knoxville, Tenn., 1969), 174–93; 191. So also John A. Yunck, calling her 'an ambiguous figure', *The Lineage of Lady Meed* (Notre Dame, Ind., 1963), 10.

true life here on earth.[20] Exactly the same statement is made, in the same terms, when Imaginatif at the end of the third dream speaks of God's 'greet mede to truthe' (XII. 292). The little allegory makes sense in its own terms—but only if you distinguish the meed to which Theology refers from the Meed of the story, as representing one of the other senses of the Middle English word. And that is no defence of Langland, for Theology plainly is referring to the Meed of the story: indeed, it is his objection that forces the marriage party to take the issue up to the king at Westminster for judgement. So one has to say that the dream fiction fails here to accommodate, as it fails also to exclude, a consideration which the usage of the word itself—its collocation with 'heaven'—evidently forced into the poet's mind.

The Middle English word also, it will be recalled, had a third focus of meaning, in addition to the bribery and the heavenly-reward senses: legitimate compensation for services rendered, wages. In this third sense the word raises an issue, or rather a cluster of issues, which exercised Langland throughout the poem, in one form or another. It is essentially a question of justice or reasonableness in the relation between what people do and what they get for what they do. In the present dream, the issue comes to a head in the dispute between Meed and Conscience before the king at Westminster. This is no 'horizontal' debate. Meed's defence of herself takes unfair advantage of the semantic range of her name and unscrupulously blurs the distinction between just and unjust rewards. In Conscience's authoritative reply, however, that distinction is decisively affirmed. Lady Meed, he argues, has no right to claim just reward as her province. Indeed, running counter to contemporary linguistic usage, he goes so far as to assert that just rewards are not 'mede' at all:

[20] The C Text makes the reference to heavenly reward clear by adding a passage in which St Lawrence on his gridiron claims to have deserved, through God's grace and mercy, his 'mede' in Heaven: C II. 132–3. It seems to follow that Schmidt must be right in understanding Amends, the mother of Meed according to Theology, as 'satisfaction for sin, which God will reward in heaven' (n. to B II. 115 in his edn.). It is one of Langland's favourite thoughts that only by making amends for their sins can men hope to win heavenly reward (e.g. XVII. 237–9). This may be represented allegorically by making (heavenly) Meed the offspring of (human) Amends.

'That laborers and lewede leodes taken of hire maistres,
It is no manere mede but a mesurable hire.'

(III. 255–6)[21]

Conscience's distinction, here in the B Text, between 'mede'
and 'mesurable hire' is a powerful one. The pregnant epithet
'mesurable' marks off that reasonable kind of reward whose
value can be measured and matched against what has been
done to deserve it. What Meed represents is therefore, by
contrast, something that Conscience calls 'mesurelees' (III.
246)—unsusceptible, that is, to rational assessment and there-
fore highly suspect to most medieval ways of thinking. How
large a bribe, after all, does a judge deserve for making an
unjust judgement?

This is a rather striking example of the way Langland's
thinking and his story-telling interact, sometimes in quite
uncomfortable ways. A story may set problems to rest, or even
appear to solve them; but it can also throw problems up.
Thus, the dispute between Conscience and Meed requires that
the latter should be firmly denied any claim to legitimacy;
but, when the term 'mede' is so restricted, how can it be
applied, as it was by Theology, to God's rewards? In the B
Text, Conscience tackles the problem directly with a scholastic
distinction. There are, he tells the king, two kinds of meed,
'two manere of medes': the corrupt one represented by Lady
Meed, and that other one which 'God of his grace graunteth
in his blisse | To tho that wel werchen while thei ben here'
(III. 231–3). But this distinction runs head-on into another
set of problems. If a 'mede' differs from other kinds of reward
by virtue of lack of measure, then it must be that God's re-
wards themselves lack measure.[22] Now this raises, accidentally

---

[21] The 'earnings' sense of the word does appear to have been less common than
the others, on the evidence of *MED* 1a (b). However, the Wycliffite Bible uses 'mede'
to render the Latin *merces* in the sense 'due reward': e.g. Tobias 12: 2, 'what meede
shul wee 3yvyn to hym?' ('quam mercedem dabimus ei?'). Such uses may have
suggested to Langland his adoption in the C Text of the neologism 'mercede' to
distinguish true rewards from false.

[22] At III. 246, Conscience introduces the second, corrupt kind of meed with the
words 'Ther is another mede mesurelees, that maistres desireth'. Stokes (*Justice and
Mercy*, 128) observes: 'The line can be read in two ways, according to whether
"mesurelees" is interpreted as predicative or attributive: "There is another kind of
meed, which is measureless (*ie* distinct from the first in being measureless)"; or, "There

as it were, what Chaucer's Friar might call a 'school-matter of great difficulty': the old question of God's justice and mercy, here in relation to individual rewards and punishments in the afterlife. It is clear that Langland does not mean to suggest that God distributes his rewards in an unreasonable or arbitrary fashion, without any regard to merit in the recipient. When Theology spoke of heavenly meed, he cited Luke's words, 'the labourer is worthy of his hire' (Luke 10: 7); and Conscience himself speaks of the good works required of those who would win heaven. Langland would surely have agreed with those fourteenth-century theologians who argued that man must 'do what in him is' to gain heavenly rewards.[23] Yet it is 'of his grace' that God grants salvation 'to tho that wel werchen while thei ben here'; for the joys of eternal life must, by their very eternal nature, be out of proportion to any human merit, however great. What is infinite cannot stand in any measurable relation to what is finite. So, as Imaginatif puts it much later, in the C Text, God shows to man 'a cortesye more þen covenant was' (C XIV. 216). But this is indeed matter for the third dream, and Langland might have done better not to raise it here. It is true that the sudden, unforeseen twist is one of the hallmarks of his allegorical fictions, and also that these twists commonly serve to drive his stories down into deeper layers of meaning. But Theology's intervention, though it raises a profound theological issue, merely confuses the story in which it occurs and obfuscates the meaning of that story—which is primarily, and properly at this point in the poem, concerned with the ethics of reward in human society.

In this respect, Langland's first dream is inferior to his second. The latter shows, I think, an increased mastery in the

---

is another kind of measureless meed (*ie* like the first in being measureless)". ' The former interpretation, however, raises the question: What have the two kinds of meed got in common (as against 'mesurable hire'), if it is not lack of measure? See James Simpson, *Piers Plowman: An Introduction to the B-Text* (London, 1990), 47–8. In their edition of B, Kane and Donaldson reject 'another' in 'another mede mesurelees', which all B manuscripts have, in favour of 'a', the reading of all A manuscripts; but this raises the same problem.

[23] On *facere quod in se est*, see William J. Courtenay, *Schools and Scholars in Fourteenth-Century England* (Princeton, NJ, 1987), 213, 294–7; and Heiko A. Oberman, *The Harvest of Medieval Theology: Gabriel Biel and Late Medieval Nominalism*, rev. edn. (Grand Rapids, Mich., 1967), 132–4.

tricky art of handling allegorical stories. It is not that the fiction of the pilgrimage to Truth proceeds in any straightforward or untroubled way, as it could easily have done in the hands of a less ambitious allegorist. The episode of the half acre, the intervention of Hunger there, the tearing by Piers of Truth's pardon, and his subsequent resolve to live a different sort of life—these all serve to divert the story from its expected course. Yet each of these moments of vision enriches meaning, as Theology's intervention does not. They are all, in fact, consummate 'fictions of the divided mind'; but I shall consider only one of them here: the episode of Piers and Hunger on the half acre.[24]

Using the term 'fiction', as I have done, may suggest that it is only in formal literary contexts that thought about general issues gets mixed up with the contemplation of imaginary cases; but this is far from the truth. Thinking about matters of behaviour or policy commonly involves the imagining of stories, situations, or 'scenarios': 'suppose someone does this . . .', 'if a person does that . . .'. Such imaginary cases may be simply exemplary—representing, that is, our sense of how things ideally ought to be. The story of the complaint of Peace against Wrong, which concludes the dream of Lady Meed, is of this exemplary kind. It is designed to show how, even in quite hard cases, justice should prevail over bribery and corruption. But stories can also serve to explore the difficulties or contradictions that may arise in the application of general principles to particular situations.[25] An example of this is the Hunger episode in Will's second dream.

In the course of Passus VI, it will be recalled, Piers the Plowman sets out to organize the people to work on his half acre. He encounters, however, a group of intransigents who sit about drinking and singing (115–16). The behaviour of these and other 'wastoures' on his field raises for Piers a difficult ethical and practical problem: in what way, if at all, should he consent to provide for such people? Langland never had

---

[24] I have previously discussed the whole dream in 'The Action of Langland's Second Vision', *Essays in Criticism*, 15 (1965), 247–68, reprinted in Blanch, *Style and Symbolism*, 209–27, and Burrow, *Essays on Medieval Literature* (Oxford, 1984), 79–101.

[25] See especially the remarkable study by Wesley Trimpi, referred to in Ch. 5 below.

any doubt, of course, that the truly deserving poor ought to
be supported; but what about the undeserving—beggars who
pretend to be crippled, and other such malingerers, as well
as the simply idle? On this matter, understandably enough,
neither he nor his age found it easy to arrive at a settled
conviction.[26] Elsewhere in the poem Langland sets out the
conflicting considerations in the form of argument *pro* and
*contra*.[27] Here on the half acre, however, he explores how such
considerations may arise as fluctuating responses to experi-
ence—responses by Piers, that is, as his anger or his pity are
successively aroused in the unfolding course of events.

His first response is one of indignant anger. Faced with the
lazy drinkers and their exasperating refrain of 'how trolly
lolly', Piers takes the hardest of hard lines. If they will not
work, let them die! Who cares?

> 'Now, by the peril of my soule!' quod Piers al in pure tene,
> 'But ye arise the rather and rape yow to werche,
> Shal no greyn that here groweth glade yow at nede,
> And though ye deye for doel, the devel have that recche!'
>
> (117–20)

This extreme position might claim the support of St Paul, 'if
any man will not work, neither let him eat' (2 Thessalonians
3: 10); but it hardly survives the 'pure tene' that prompted it.
Coming down to earth, Piers soon recognizes that something
after all must be done to keep the wasters, even if they refuse
to work, from actually dying: 'ye shul eten barly breed and

---

[26] Relevant studies are: Donaldson, *The C-Text and its Poet*, 130–6; Derek Pearsall,
'Poverty and Poor People in *Piers Plowman*', in E. D. Kennedy, R. Waldron, and J.
S. Wittig (eds.), *Medieval English Studies Presented to George Kane* (Woodbridge, 1988),
167–85; David Aers, *Community, Gender, and Individual Identity: English Writing 1360–1430*
(London, 1988), ch. 1. For an account of the canon lawyers' uncertain treatment of
the matter, see Brian Tierney, *Medieval Poor Law* (Berkeley and Los Angeles, 1959),
ch. 3, 'Charity'.

[27] For example, in his commentary on the pardon sent by Truth, B VII. 64–97
(C IX. 61–174), discussing the question of whether beggars ought to be supported
without regard to their circumstances. Here the B Text cites authorities on both sides
of the question: Cato and Comestor are in favour of discrimination in the dispensing
of charity, but (*ac*) Gregory is against. B inclines to the latter view, with the proviso
that the bogus poor who enjoy the benefits of indiscriminate charity will be held
to account by God. The C Text quotes only Cato ('*Cui des, videto*', IX. 69) and
favours his view, even suggesting at one point that malingerers may be left to starve
(IX. 101).

of the broke drynke' (135). Coarse bread and water will serve to keep body and soul together. There follows, however, another outburst of anger as Piers, infuriated by the continued obstinacy and impertinence of the wasters, summons Hunger to take vengeance on them:

'Now, by the peril of my soule!' quod Piers, 'I shal apeire
    yow alle'—
And houped after Hunger, that herde hym at the firste.
'Awreke me of thise wastours,' quod he, 'that this world shendeth!'
                                                    (171-3)

Hunger accordingly launches a savagely vengeful assault on the layabouts, bringing them close to the point of death.[28] Yet the actual sight of starvation prompts in Piers a new sense of sympathy and concern. He begs Hunger to stop: let the wasters live, he asks, at least on coarse bread or pig-food (181-2). And when this regime provokes the idlers to work, their frenzied but ill-rewarded efforts inspire in Piers first pride (197) and then pity (199). He asks Hunger to leave, and even begins to wonder whether harsh measures may not be inconsistent with the teachings of Christ:

'. . . it are my blody bretheren, for God boughte us alle.
Truthe taughte me ones to loven hem ech one
And to helpen hem of alle thyng, ay as hem nedeth.'
                                                    (207-9)

These potent words express a doctrine of unrestricted and undiscriminating charity which recalls Christ's command: 'Give to every one that asketh thee' (Luke 6: 30).

Thus, two conflicting strains in biblical teaching find expression dramatically in the shifting responses of Piers, his 'tene' and his 'pite'. On the one hand, St Paul: 'if any man will not work, neither let him eat'; on the other, Christ: 'Give to every one that asketh thee'. It is another version of the perennial conflict between justice and mercy. Turning to Hunger for advice in his perplexity, Piers is offered

---

[28] On the significance of Hunger, as representing annual shortages, crop failures, and famines, see R. W. Frank, 'The "Hungry Gap", Crop Failure, and Famine: The Fourteenth-Century Agricultural Crisis and *Piers Plowman*', *Yearbook of Langland Studies*, 4 (1990), 87-104.

reassurance: it is indeed right to discriminate between the truly disadvantaged and the frauds, and to support the latter only with the very barest necessities of life.[29] Yet he is still not entirely convinced:

'I wolde noght greve God,' quod Piers, 'for al the good on grounde!
Mighte I synnelees do as thow seist?' seide Piers thanne.

(229–30)

In an effort to set his mind at rest, Hunger cites a battery of supporting texts, from Genesis, Wisdom, Matthew, and the Psalms.

The doctrine of minimal life-support for malingerers may seem a rather harsh one today; but in the Hunger episode it figures as a somewhat unstable compromise between the extremes of justice (let them die if they will not work) and mercy (let them eat with the rest of us). The two opposing views are represented in the narrative in the changing reactions of Piers, faced as he is on the one hand by the maddening spectacle of arrogant parasitism, and on the other by the saddening spectacle of starvation. What the story shows most vividly is how opinions in such matters are swayed by changing circumstances and by the shifting feelings that they arouse.

For a last example of a 'fiction of the divided mind' I turn to the dinner party at the house of Conscience in Passus XIII. This masterly scene illustrates better than any other how a swirling mass of mixed feelings and conflicting thoughts may be set at rest or fixed in the right kind of imagined narrative. The feelings and thoughts in question have boiled up with increasing turbulence in the course of the long preceding dream. At the beginning of that dream, in Passus VIII, Long Will set out in search of knowledge—knowledge of Dowel; and the story which ensues, such as it is, consists of a series of encounters with persons representing the various powers, activities, and instruments of the thinking mind. The chief

[29] Hunger's words at VI. 225–6a conflict with the general tenor of his advice to Piers, for they plainly advocate indiscriminate charity, leaving distinctions between the deserving and undeserving to the judgement of God. They are not present in the A Text and are omitted in C: see Donaldson, *The C-Text and its Poet*, 131–2, and Aers, *Community, Gender, and Individual Identity*, 45–6.

business of this whole section is to unpack and examine intellectually the content of what was given in visionary form in the pardon sent by Truth: the promise, or hope, that virtuous living (Dowel) wins a place in heaven. Many questions now arise for discussion. What is Dowel? And is it true, in any case, that 'those who have done good things will go into eternal life'? Are God's ways indeed so just and reasonable? What, then, about the doctrine of predestination? And what of the righteous heathen? Do they gain salvation? To such questions Will is offered extensive answers by his various instructors, but he is by no means satisfied with what he hears. For one thing, he does not always agree, and is inclined to argue points. He is himself a clerk and can play the intellectual game, with *contra*s and *ergo*s: ' "*Contra!*" quod I as a clerc, and comsed to disputen' (VIII. 20). Yet he also expresses, more incoherently, a deeper dissatisfaction. He recalls that Christ himself never said anything to encourage such discussions, for he never favoured the learned, the intellectual, or the academic: 'Clergie of Cristes mouth comended was it nevere' (X. 440).[30] What Will claims to be looking for is a different sort of knowledge, which he calls 'kynde knowynge'. His response to the teaching of Thought is typical:

I thonked Thoght tho that he me so taughte.
'Ac yet savoreth me noght thi seying, so me Crist helpe!
For more kynde knowynge I coveite to lerne—
How Dowel, Dobet and Dobest doon among the peple.'

(VIII. 109–12)

The verb 'savour' appeals to the sense of taste, as if Will were looking for the kind of knowledge which could be received as directly and unmistakably as tastes are by the palate, a 'kynde' or natural knowledge.[31] It is also a knowledge associated

[30] 'Nevere' is the reading of the A Text. All B manuscripts read 'litel' here, but Schmidt and Kane–Donaldson read with A. C rewrites to clarify. The passage evidently troubled scribes, perhaps because they disliked what it said.
[31] See M. C. Davlin, '*Kynde Knowynge* as a Major Theme in *Piers Plowman* B', *RES* NS 22 (1971), 1–19. Langland's use of 'savoreth' here perhaps harks back to the origins of the Latin *sapientia*, 'wisdom', correctly understood by medieval scholars as related etymologically to *sapor*, 'flavour'. Thus Isidore of Seville: '*Sapiens* is so called after *sapor*; for just as taste is able to distinguish the flavour of foods, so the wise man is able to discriminate between things and issues', *Etymologiae*, ed. W. M. Lindsay (Oxford, 1911), X. 240.

immediately with action: he wants to know how Dowel and the rest *do* among the people. Moral theology is all very well, but its subtle argumentations seem to have little practical effect, even on the theologians themselves.

It is not easy to know quite what to make of this. It must be right for Will to desire a knowledge of Dowel which leads to virtuous action rather than academic debate. Indeed Dame Study herself, one of his academic instructors, makes that very point even more forcefully than Will, in her attack on frivolous disputation: 'And tho that useth thise havylons to ablende mennes wittes | What is Dowel fro Dobet, now deef mote he worthe' (X. 131–2). Yet the very fact that Study can herself speak in these terms suggests that Will's attack on the learned disciplines may be partial and unfair. He does not have a monopoly of wisdom. Indeed, in the quasi-autobiographical inner dream in Passus XI, he learns that his depreciation of 'clergye' has its source not in wisdom but in pride (XI. 15–16); and when he wakes from this dream, Imaginatif reiterates the charge:

> 'Pryde now and presumpcion paraventure wol thee appele,
> That Clergie thi compaignye ne kepeth noght to suwe.'
>
> (XI. 421–2)

Dame Study had earlier promised that Will's doubts about clerkly wisdom would be answered by Imaginatif, and the latter does indeed address himself to the question, in the last long speech of the third dream. What he offers Will is something like a balanced account of the matter, with the help of a few *ac*s. Knowledge, he says, is a heavenly thing, but (*ac*) grace is a mystery that no clerk can fathom, but (*ac*) clergy is commendable, especially 'clergie for Cristes love' (XII. 64–71). When Will spoke his crabbed words against the learned, he was right about some, but wrong about others (156–60).[32] And so on. The speech concludes the dream on a note of sound common sense, defending what can reasonably be defended in its distinctive world of intellectual activity. Yet

---

[32] Imaginatif refers in particular to Will's contention that ignorant men are actually more likely than the learned to win salvation—the culmination of his tirade in Passus X (453–72a). In the C Text these remarks are transferred to Rechelesnesse, perhaps in an attempt to make their dubious status clearer.

the settlement offered by Imaginatif is hardly satisfactory, or
so Langland seems to have thought; for in the ensuing scene
of the dinner party he sets out to educe a proper attitude to
'clergy' in a different fashion, by creating a fiction in which
that attitude is not defined but displayed.

This scene is much more richly imagined than any of the
rather shadowy encounters with Thought and the rest. Con-
science invites Will to dinner at his residence, in company
with Clergy. As Derek Pearsall observes, the invitation is in
the nature of a 'probationary reward for Will, who has shown
recent signs of improvement'.[33] Although Imaginatif had said
that Clergy no longer wanted to have anything to do with
Will, he has now evidently relented; but Will and Clergy do
not exactly meet at the dinner. The hall at Conscience's
'court' is arranged like the hall of a modern Oxbridge college,
with a high table on a dais across one end for the more
distinguished guests, and 'side boards' running the length of
the hall for the rest.[34] Clergy sits at high table with his host,
in company with the most honoured guest, a learned friar.
Lower down the hall, at a side table, sits Will, sharing dishes
with another diner, as one did in the Middle Ages. His 'mette'
or dinner-companion is a new character, the poor pilgrim
Patience, who has recently appeared as a beggar in Con-
science's courtyard and been hospitably received. Will has
evidently been put firmly in his place:

> Pacience and I were put to be mettes,
> And seten bi oureselve at a side borde.   (XIII. 35–6)

Dinner parties commonly figure among allegorical episodes
in the religious dream poetry of the time, as in the French
*Songe d'Enfer* and *Songe de Paradis*, where dreamers are enter-
tained to several such occasions. But I know of no poem where
the scene is developed so vividly and subtly to express rela-
tionships between the various *signifiés* of the allegory. Admit-
tedly, it may at first seem that the vexed question of clerical
learning is to be settled in summary fashion, for the learned
friar fulfils, in gross and lurid caricature, all Will's darkest
suspicions. The friar can say good things about Dowel—he

---

[33] Note to C XV. 26–7 in his edition.   [34] Compare XII. 198–201.

is, after all, a *magister* and a *doctor*—but is also an evident hypocrite and glutton. Friars were notorious in Langland's time for liking to sit at the high table; and this predilection was enough, in the eyes of their enemies, to identify them with the hypocritical scribes and Pharisees of whom Christ said, 'they love the first places at feasts and the first chairs in the synagogues'.[35] The present friar is also a greedy eater, with a fat paunch and cheeks 'as rody as a rose'. Clearly the moral advantage here lies with Will, who shares with Patience spiritual foods, eating texts from the penitential psalms, while the friar consumes puddings, game, tripe, and fried eggs.

Yet the matter is not quite so simple, for although Patience rejoices in their penitential fare, Will is far from happy with it:

> Pacience was proude of that propre service,
> And made hym murthe with his mete; ac I mornede evere,
> For this doctour on the heighe dees drank wyn so faste.
>
> (XII. 58–60)

In his edition of the B Text, Schmidt well translates the word 'mornede' here as 'sulked'. Will has, of course, good reasons for moral indignation, and these he goes on to express in a *sotto-voce* soliloquy overheard (as it is designed to be) by his companion: XIII. 63–84. This very friar, this 'God's glutton', has preached in London on the theme of penitential suffering; but he does not practise what he preaches; so here is a notable instance of that divorce between word and deed, suspicion of which haunted the third dream. Yet Will's motives for his anger are far from pure. He feels as many undergraduates have felt, looking up at the good living on the high table and conscious of their own no doubt superior merit. Or as Julien Sorel feels, in Stendhal's *Scarlet and Black*, as a clever young tutor in the bourgeois household of M. de Rênal: 'Pour lui, il n'éprouvait que haine et horreur pour la haute société où il était admis, à la vérité au bas bout de la table, ce qui explique peut-être la haine et l'horreur.'[36]

---

[35] Matt. 23: 6. See Penn R. Szittya, *The Antifraternal Tradition in Medieval Literature* (Princeton, NJ, 1986), 37–8, 77, 202.

[36] 'He felt nothing but loathing and abhorrence for the distinguished company into which he had been admitted (though only, it has to be said, to the very bottom end of the table, which may perhaps explain the loathing and the abhorrence)', *Le Rouge et le noir*, Bk. I, ch. 7.

Will is not a character in a novel, however. He is indeed a person, as the present episode itself shows; but he is also a personification, of the human will, *voluntas*, and, here as often, of the wilfulness which the will is inclined to display. So, for a model response to the provocation that the friar represents, one must combine Will with Patience, and include their host Conscience. For conscience is the faculty and patience the virtue which may control and direct impetuous human reactions in such a case. Overhearing Will's angry soliloquy, accordingly, Patience gives his companion a sharp restraining look ('preynte on me to be stille', XIII. 85): wait till the friar has finished eating, he suggests, before addressing any remarks to him. Will obeys; and when the friar has finished his meal and started talking, Conscience raises with him the old question of the three lives and glances down the hall towards Patience and Will as if to invite their participation in the symposium. Will can therefore with a good conscience ask his customary question, which he does quite politely: 'What is Dowel, sire doctour... is Dobest any penaunce?' The provocation, such as it is, lies in the reference to penance; but the friar replies with a perfectly respectable definition of Dowel: 'Do noon yvel to thyn evencristen'. Will, however, can barely contain his indignation, and he replies with words in which anger is thinly disguised as sociable jocularity:

'By this day, sire doctour,' quod I, 'thanne in Dowel be ye noght!
For ye han harmed us two in that ye eten the puddyng.'

(XIII. 105–6)

This is the cue for Conscience to give the third of the scene's speaking looks, directed this time at Patience. The courteous host wants his unruly guest restrained:

Thanne Conscience ful curteisly a contenaunce he made,
And preynte upon Pacience to preie me to be stille.

(111–12)[37]

[37] 'Preynte', here and at XIII. 85 (where it is a conjectural reading) and XVIII. 21, denotes some kind of warning glance directed at Will, like the 'egre' or sharp look which Piers shoots at him elsewhere (XVI. 64). At such moments Langland is evidently in full imaginative possession of his story-world. An amusing example is X. 137–43. Here Wit has been ticked off by his wife Study for wasting words on Will: 'He bicom so confus he kouthe noght loke.' So, when Will persists in begging for further

Accordingly, we hear no more from Will in the scene.

The effect of the story so far is to enforce upon Will the lesson which he was taught in the inner dream of Passus XI, the lesson of patience or 'suffraunce'. Faced here with the grossest example of all that he most objects to in the academic intelligentsia, he must struggle to contain his abhorrence. Although Will's indignation is not unmixed with envy and resentment, he is clearly right to condemn the friar: there can be no question of a divided mind about him. However, there is also at the dinner party another representative of the learned professions, Clergy himself; and here matters are not so straightforward. The position of Clergy is defined, in the latter part of the scene, in relation to the undoubted hero of the hour, Patience; and the definition turns out to be a subtle and balanced one. The story here serves, in fact, to articulate Langland's mixed feelings about the intellectual establishment better than any number of Imaginatif's *acs*; and it proves to represent, in effect, his last word on the subject.

After the friar has made his contribution to the Dowel symposium, Conscience turns to Clergy for his opinion; and his response has none of the glib alacrity which was so offensive in the friar. He lacks, he says, the confidence to pronounce on the matter at all until he has had the opportunity to consult his seven sons (the seven liberal arts); for one Piers the Plowman 'hath impugned us alle, | And set alle sciences at a sop save love one'.[38] To be impugned by Piers Plowman is no light matter, but Clergy's response is, in its way, exemplary. He reserves the right to pronounce at some future time, but only after anxious consultations prompted by the evangelical simplicity of Piers's challenge. He is aware of the limitations of the learned disciplines that he represents, and open to voices from beyond their range. To be aware of

---

explanations, he responds only with a laugh, a bow, and a look: 'al laughynge he louted and loked upon Studie | In signe that I sholde bisechen hire of grace'. There is a humorous appeal to male solidarity in this act of deference.

[38] XIII. 123–24. In the C Text, Piers Plowman himself, not otherwise present at the dinner, suddenly speaks and then vanishes: XV. 138–50. Pearsall calls this a 'mysterious and dramatic appearance' (n. to line 138 in his edn.); but it seems to me to betray an unfortunate tendency in the C revision to treat the literal story with insufficient respect.

one's limitations, however, is not the same as transcending them; and when Conscience turns from Clergy to Patience, he looks for something more:

'Pacience hath be in many place, and paraunter knoweth
That no clerk ne kan, as Crist bereth witnesse'.

(XIII. 133–4)

Patience, the poor pilgrim, responds with a speech on the 'science' of love which, in its enthusiasm and riddling obscurity, does set love above all intellectual disciplines: learning is good, he says, and teaching is better, but love is best of all, Dobest. This utterance from the body of the hall provokes a variety of responses from the high table. The friar dismisses it as idealistic claptrap; but Conscience is touched, and declares his intention of leaving the dinner party (even though he is the host) and joining Patience on his pilgrimage. Clergy, however, cannot approve this decision, and he offers Conscience his own alternative discipline:

'I shal brynge yow a bible, a book of the olde lawe,
And lere yow, if yow like, the leeste point to knowe,
That Pacience the pilgrym parfitly knew nevere.'

(185–7)

The limitations of Clergy are firmly—perhaps too firmly— marked here. His reference to a book of the old law suggests that the new law of love may not figure in those authorities to which he is wedded, and his offer to expound even 'the least point' to his pupil perhaps savours of pedantry.

Yet Clergy is no scribe or Pharisee, and his farewell exchanges with Conscience, as the latter prepares to set off with Patience, quietly but firmly defend the rights and duties of the clerisy, in face of Conscience's kindled enthusiasm for perfection.[39] To Patience's parting declaration that he would

---

[39] In the C Text, Langland omitted B XIII. 202–14, thus depriving Clergy of his response to Conscience, and leaving the balance tipped heavily against him. Clergy's final standing also suffers there from the two lines added after Conscience's reference to his pack of books: '"Lettrure and longe studie letteth fol monye, | That they knoweth nat," quod Concience, "what is kynde Pacience" ' (C XV. 181–2). In addition, the reference to perfection is shifted from Clergy's mouth to Conscience's (B XIII. 214, C XV. 184), and so loses its ironic resonance. The simplification of the fiction entails a simplification also in the thought.

rather 'have pacience parfitliche than half thi pak of bokes',
Clergy responds gravely:

> 'Thow shalt se the tyme
> Whan thow art wery forwalked, wilne me to counseille.'
>
> (203–4)

This could be mistaken for, but is not, the weary or cynical
voice of experience. In fact, Conscience himself acknowledges
the justice of Clergy's prediction ('That is sooth'), as if recog-
nizing that one cannot in the long term live entirely on
enthusiasm; but as he goes on to imagine a future when Clergy
will join him in an ideal partnership with Patience, he kindles
again:

> 'If Pacience be oure partyng felawe and pryve with us bothe,
> Ther nys wo in this world that we ne sholde amende,
> And conformen kynges to pees, and alle kynnes londes—
> Sarsens and Surre, and so forth alle the Jewes—
> Turne into the trewe feith and intil oon bileve.'
>
> (206–10)

It is a splendid vision, but one to which Clergy administers a
final check:

> 'That is sooth,' quod Clergie, 'I se what thow menest.
> I shall dwelle as I do, my devoir to shewe,
> And confermen fauntekyns oother folk ylered
> Til Pacience have preved thee and parfit thee maked.'
>
> (211–14)

Clergy does see what Conscience means; but his final refer-
ence to perfection is lightly touched with irony, as the word
'parfit' so often is in *Piers Plowman*. It is not easy to be perfect.
There is a gentle irony too in 'confermen fauntekyns', a phrase
which pointedly echoes Conscience's grander 'conformen kyn-
ges to pees', and so affirms the more mundane 'devoirs' or
duties which it is surely not wrong for the clerisy to persist
in. There is no question of a triumph for Clergy here:
Conscience, as he sets off with Patience, carries the poem with
him. Yet neither is Clergy a mere clerical organization man,
for established learning does have its part to play. The fiction
here perfectly expresses both sides of the case.

# CHAPTER 3

# Fictions of History

Anyone who set out to read *Piers Plowman* for the story might well end up, like the reader of Richardson imagined by Dr Johnson, so much fretted that he would hang himself. Separation of dream from dream breaks up the narrative continuity of the whole, and what in the last chapter I described as Langland's divided mind and mixed feelings serve further to trouble the orderly progress of events towards any satisfactory end. Yet if one stands far enough back from the poem one can see, in its deeper structure, a pattern of three successive controlling narratives. In the first of these, the subject is society, as Langland saw it in the England of his day; and the action expresses, in the stories of Lady Meed and of the pilgrimage to Truth, the poet's hopes and fears concerning that society's future reformation. In the poem's middle phase, extending from B VIII to XV, the focus is upon an individual, Long Will; and the action charts his very uncertain progress towards understanding both of God's world and of himself. In the third and last phase, the subject is mankind, and the controlling narrative is historical. From Passus XVI to the end, that is, the poem follows an order dictated by the history of man's salvation. This is the history with which the present chapter will be concerned: the history of salvation, *heilsgeschichte*, as it was recorded and prophesied in the Bible, and as it was known from the history of the Church since biblical times. These were, of course, no fictions for Langland himself—on the contrary, they were for him the essence of history—but when Will dreams of these events in the poem they become, in certain interesting ways, fictionalized.

It is not difficult to see how, from Passus XVI on, salvation-history dictates the order of events—though not without some characteristic delays and diversions on the way. The poem keeps its tryst with history at the Tree of Charity. Will sees this tree first as a timeless—or, as they said in the Middle Ages, 'quotidian'—symbol of the moral life, representing the

supremacy of charity among the virtues. As such, it belongs
with what has gone before. Will's education in the virtues, in
the middle phase of the poem, has led him through Dowel
and patience to that supreme virtue which the tree called
Patience bears as its fruit in good men's hearts: 'Patience hatte
the pure tree, and pore symple of herte, | And so thorugh
God and thorugh goode men groweth the fruyt Charite'
(XVI. 8–9). There is no call to think of history here. Yet by
the end of the scene the tree has come to stand, not for the
conclusion of a moral sequence, but for the beginning of a
historical one. This crucial moment of transition is handled
with extraordinary freedom and audacity. Will, who still
hankers after that direct, unmediated knowledge which he has
been looking for throughout the preceding section, sees the
opportunity of actually sinking his teeth into a virtue and
tasting its 'savour' for himself; so he asks Piers Plowman to
fetch him down an apple from the tree. But as Piers shakes
the tree in order to dislodge one, a sinister and dreamlike
transformation takes place. The tree cries out, and as the
apples fall—

> evere as thei dropped adoun the devel was redy,
> And gadrede hem alle togideres, bothe grete and smale—
> Adam and Abraham and Ysaye the prophete,
> Sampson and Samuel, and Seint Johan the Baptist;
> Bar hem forth boldely—no body hym letted—
> And made of holy men his hoord *in Limbo Inferni*,
> There is derknesse and drede and the devel maister.
>
> (XVI. 79–85)

These startling lines plunge the reader quite suddenly into the
time of the Old Testament, and into a history at the beginning
of which, we now realize, a fruit tree has its own proper place.
Certainly Long Will's persistent desire for 'kind knowing' may
here be seen as a legacy of the first; fatal curiosity of Adam
and Eve; but that is no longer the main point. The tree now
comes to stand for that great event itself, without which the
history of salvation would never have needed to happen. It is
for the same reason that, in Deguileville's *Pelerinage de Jhesucrist*,
the poet's dream of the life of Christ begins with a vision of
an old man climbing an apple tree, eating its fruit, and falling

to the earth.[1] In Deguileville, the earth opens and swallows
the man up; in Langland, the devil carries off the fruit and
stores it in his 'hoord' in Limbo.[2] The significance is the same
in each case. Furthermore, in Langland's list of Old Testa-
ment names, the first and the last, Adam and John the Baptist,
precisely bracket the whole span of time before Christ, from
the Fall to the Redemption.

So perhaps readers should not be as surprised as they always
are when the vision of the Tree of Charity gives place, in the
immediately following lines, to a vision of the Annunciation:

> And thanne spak *Spiritus Sanctus* in Gabrielis mouthe
> To a maide that highte Marie, a meke thyng withalle.
>
> (XVI. 90–1)

Yet it is surely a thrilling moment. The temporal adverb
'thanne' boldly identifies this moment in the inner dream with
the historical moment when God first became man—as hap-
pened precisely at the Annunciation, nine months before the
birth of Christ. And it seems appropriate that the poem's
decisive junction with history—decisive, that is, for the whole
of the rest of its course—should take just this form: for the
first time in all his visions, Will actually sees (as distinct from
hearing about) a biblical event; and what he sees, represented
not allegorically but with a certain simple directness, is the
moment when God became flesh and dwelt among us. It is
as if the poem's entry into history imitates God's own sudden
and decisive entry at the Incarnation.

What follows is less well handled. The account of Christ's
life up to the moment of his arrest in Gethsemane, which
occupies the rest of the inner dream, maintains the poem's
newly acquired historical impetus; but the fact that one must
call it an account rather than a vision suggests a weakness, to
which I shall return shortly. Also, there is a certain awkward-
ness when the poem, after breaking off the inner dream on
the eve of Good Friday, resumes its main dream with a second
build-up to the Crucifixion, plunging the reader back into
Old Testament times. Yet this second build-up is itself well

---

[1] *Pelerinage de Jhesucrist*, lines 65–74. See also Appendix A.
[2] 'Hoord' is a word elsewhere associated with fruit, as in Chaucer's 'hoord of apples
leyd in hey or heeth', *Canterbury Tales*, I. 3262.

managed, in a much more convincingly visionary mode than
the first. The three figures in the vision represent the Pauline
triad faith, hope, and charity, 'and the greatest of these is
charity'; but Langland projects these on to the screen of
history by identifying them with another traditional triad, that
of the three successive ages of law. Faith, in the person of
Abraham, represents the first of these ages, before the recep-
tion of the Ten Commandments, when men lived according
to a natural law written, as St Paul puts it, 'in their hearts'
(Romans 2: 15). Hope, in the person of Moses, represents the
Old Law and carries the Commandments (or rather Christ's
summary of them) on a piece of hard rock. Finally, the Good
Samaritan represents the supreme virtue of charity, the New
Law of love. The vision of these three hurrying towards
Christ's great joust at Jerusalem as if to a Cup Final generates
a powerful narrative momentum, only partially dispelled by
some overlong speeches. The sense of expectation felt by these
precursors is fulfilled when, at the beginning of Passus XVIII,
the Samaritan becomes identified with Christ himself—the
Christ of the Entry into Jerusalem.

From this point onwards, the poem follows its historical
course more straightforwardly, albeit in a highly selective
fashion. Passus XVIII re-enacts the events of the Passion as
described in the Gospels and the Apocrypha: the trial, the
Crucifixion, the Harrowing of Hell, and the Resurrection.
Passus XIX draws on the Acts of the Apostles for its version
of the descent of the Holy Spirit at Pentecost and the first
establishment of the Church under St Peter. Finally, this vision
of the charismatic early Church is contrasted with Langland's
bleak vision of its successor in his own day—a Church which
has somehow mysteriously lost its pristine potency. Unlike
Dante in *Purgatorio* 32, Langland does not attempt to depict
the process of this deterioration. Instead, he simply juxtaposes
the two contrary states—'look here upon this picture, and on
this'—and thus completes his historical sequence, which began
in the Garden of Eden, with a rapid return to the present
day. But his treatment of the fourteenth-century Church
suggests, I think, that he had in mind a version of ecclesiastical
decline, current in his day, according to which the Church
suffered first from persecutors, then from heretics, and then,

worst of all, from hypocrites; for it is hypocrisy, and especially the hypocrisy of the friars, that he represents as the chief enemy in his own day, insidiously corrupting the Church from within.[3] Friar Flatterer 'enchants' the men of Holy Church; and that friar's name, 'Penetrans Domos', is enough to hint that the end of history is approaching, for it alludes to Paul's prophecy of the last days, when men 'having an appearance indeed of godliness but denying the power thereof... creep into houses [*penetrant domos*] and lead captive silly women laden with sins'.[4] So Langland's historical sequence comes to an end at a point somewhere near the end of history itself.

This account of the historical sequence, however, is open to objections: that it makes the third phase of *Piers Plowman* sound too much like those poetic paraphrases of the Bible which were commonly produced in the Middle Ages; and that, in any case, versions of biblical story appear also in Langland's poem elsewhere and are by no means peculiar to this last part of it. Both these objections can be met, I think, by distinguishing between two distinct ways of introducing biblical story into the narrative—as the poet himself quite consistently does in practice. It is a question of whether or not the Bible events are incorporated into the fictive world of the poem—its 'story-space', or what Gérard Genette calls the 'diegesis'.[5] An example of a passage where there is no such incorporation may be seen in the story of Cain and Noah told by Wit in Passus IX. This narrative belongs within the story-space of the dream only in so far as the dream-figure Wit tells it to Will: it is not like, say, Hamlet's narrative of his voyage to England, which describes off-stage events in the fiction itself. Cain and Noah are not, in that sense, off-stage characters in

---

[3] See Penn R. Szittya, *The Antifraternal Tradition in Medieval Literature* (Princeton, NJ, 1986), 33–4, on the Three Persecutions of the Church, as expounded by the *Glossa Ordinaria* commenting on ch. 6 of Rev. (the four horses of the apocalypse). A similar historical scheme was derived from Ps. 90: 5–6 (AV 91: 5–6), according to which the third, modern age was again identified as an age of hypocrisy: Bernard of Clairvaux, *Sermones super Cantica Canticorum 1–35*, ed. J. Leclercq, C. H. Talbot, and H. M. Rochais (Rome, 1957), Sermo 33, pp. 243–4.

[4] 2 Tim. 3: 5–6. See Szittya, *Antifraternal Tradition*, 58–61.

[5] 'Story-space' is an expression of Seymour Chatman's: *Story and Discourse: Narrative Structure in Fiction and Film* (Ithaca, NY, 1978), 96. On diegesis, see the excellent study by Gérard Genette, *Narrative Discourse* (Oxford, 1980), 27.

Will's dream, as is Truth in his second dream, for instance. Truth belongs to the fictive world there, even though Will never sees him; but Cain and Noah belong, as Genette puts it, on a different narrative level.[6] Even more obvious is the contrast with figures who actually appear on-stage in the story, such as Abraham in XVI or Christ in XVIII. In reporting his dreams, Langland claims to be 'saying as I saw', and Christ and Abraham are among those that he actually sees.[7]

In treating biblical history within his story-space, Langland generally observes certain special rules—rules which do not apply at the other narrative level. One obvious requirement is that events which are reported as actually occurring in the dreams should be such that they could conceivably be seen. Clearly, ordinary common-sense rules of probability do not apply here—one may see all sorts of strange things in dream— but there are limits beyond which, especially in summary narrative, one ceases to imagine the events as seen at all. Coleridge recognized this, in his objection to a passage in the dream allegory of John Bunyan. The passage from *Pilgrim's Progress* runs as follows: 'Then I saw that one came to Passion, and brought him a bag of treasure, and poured it down at his feet; the which he took up, and rejoiced therein, and withal laughed Patience to scorn; but I beheld but a while, and he had lavished all away, and had nothing left him but rags.'[8] Coleridge objected to this as an instance of 'faulty allegory': 'The beholding "but a while", and the change into "nothing

[6] *Narrative Discourse*, 227–34. Genette would assign the Cain–Noah narrative to his second type of metadiegetic narrative, where there is 'no spatio-temporal continuity between metadiegesis and diegesis' (p. 233).

[7] Langland twice speaks of 'saying as I saw': 'Of this matere I myghte mamelen ful longe, | Ac I shal seye as I saugh, so me God helpe' (B V. 21–2); 'A litel y over-leep for lesynges sake, | That y ne sygge nat as y syhe, suynde my teme' (C XX. 357–8). The poet was evidently himself aware, as every reader must be, of the distinction in his work between vision and digressive 'mameling'. The latter—going on about things—may be justified by its didactic value ('for lesynges sake', that is, in order to make a point about lying); but the former has higher authority. Compare C XI. 152–3:'And þe trewe trinite to Austyn apperede | And he us saide as he sey, and so y bileve.'

[8] *The Pilgrim's Progress*, ed. J. B. Wharey and R. Sharrock, 2nd edn. (Oxford, 1960), 31. For Coleridge's comment, see *Coleridge on the Seventeenth Century*, ed. Roberta F. Brinkley (Durham, NC, 1955), 478. I think now that I was wrong to treat this comment as 'purely Neo-Classical' in my *Essays on Medieval Literature* (Oxford, 1984), 207.

but rags" is not legitimately imaginable. A longer time and more interlinks are requisite.' When he calls this episode 'not legitimately imaginable', Coleridge must mean that one cannot imagine the events described, without the requisite time and interlinks, being *seen*, even in a dream: how could one, even there, 'behold but a while' and see someone squander a fortune? This is a valid objection. In Deguileville's dream version of the life of Christ, the *Pelerinage de Jhesucrist*, there are several such passages, especially in the section describing Christ's ministry, where the sense of things seen in a vision is lost, and one is left with flatly straightforward biblical paraphrase. Langland runs the same risk in that summary account of Christ's life up to his arrest which follows the Tree of Charity episode in Passus XVI. Here too 'a longer time and more interlinks are requisite'—so much so, in fact, that one critic quite fails to remember that Will is actually said to see these events. For she writes: 'in explaining the meaning of the tree [of Charity], Piers tells the dreamer the story of the life of Jesus and then vanishes'.[9] It is a mistake, but an understandable one. Although the events in question are in fact seen by Will, the narrative mode is one suited, not to vision, but to that other 'level' where, as in Wit's account of Cain and Noah, events are not shown but told, and where any number of interlinks may therefore be omitted.

This distinction between two levels of biblical narrative raises a matter of particular significance for the present study: the question, or problem, of treating biblical history as fiction. It is sometimes suggested that medieval writers were not particularly sensitive to the distinction between fiction and fact, story and history;[10] but this is certainly not the case with those writers in whose tradition Langland chiefly stands: the French authors of religious dream poems. Commonly rhyming *songe* with *mençonge*, these writers frankly contrast the lying or fabulous nature of their literary dreams with the 'verité pur'

---

[9] Ruth M. Ames, *The Fulfillment of the Scriptures: Abraham, Moses, and Piers* (Evanston, Ill., 1970), 178. A naïve case of the interchange between events narrated in a dream and events seen there may be found in the second part of *Pilgrim's Progress*: Sagacity describes to the dreamer the first stage of Christiana's story, but then 'left me to Dream out my Dream by myself' (ed. cit. 188).

[10] e.g. J. A. Burrow, *Medieval Writers and their Work* (Oxford, 1982), 15–17.

of Holy Scripture. The contrast is baldly stated by the author of the thirteenth-century *Songe de Paradis*. Here the dreamer has woken from a vision of heaven and an encounter with God himself:

> Lors m'esvillai, si me dolu
> Li cuers pour che que je par songe
> —Que n'estoit point voirs, mais mençonge—
> Avoie en Paradis esté.
> Petit m'i avoit on fiesté.
> Mais pour che que j'ai tant songié,
> De dire songes prenc congié,
> Si dirai fine verité.[11]

Accordingly, the poet goes on to speak of Paradise without recourse to poetic fiction, following Scripture and St Bernard of Clairvaux. Guillaume de Deguileville addresses the same matter rather more subtly, at the end of each of his three poems, and especially after waking from his dream of the pilgrimage of the soul. One expects *mençonge* from a *songe*, he says, and he will positively 'affirm' only those parts of the foregoing dream which directly represent revealed truth; but the dream has taught him to abandon worldly pleasures and prepare for death, and in that deeper sense it has not lied.[12]

Langland himself never addresses the matter so directly; but the treatment of biblical history in *Piers Plowman* clearly displays his awareness of the fictivity of a dream world. He has, in fact, two quite distinct modes of treating biblical events, according to whether they occur within or outside the poem's fictive story-space. In cases of the latter kind, such as the story of Cain and Noah, Langland adopts an essentially literal

[11] 'Then I woke up, and my heart was heavy that I had been in Paradise only in dream—for it was not true, but a lie. I enjoyed very little hospitality there. But, having dreamed so much, I shall report dreams no more, but say the plain truth'. *Le Songe de Paradis*, ed. A. Scheler, *Trouvères Belges*, nouvelle série (Louvain, 1879), lines 1026–33.
[12] *Le Pelerinage de l'Ame*, lines 11022–41. Compare *Pelerinage de Jhesucrist*, lines 11191–7; and *Pelerinage de Vie Humaine*, lines 13521–6. Deguileville revised and expanded this last passage in the second version of the poem. Where the first version simply explains that one cannot expect dreams to be all true and disowns any error that may be found in the poem, the revised text introduces the traditional image of grain and chaff, urging the reader to store the one and discard the other: Vérard ed. (Paris, 1511), p. cvi recto.

method. That is, he will do nothing more than fill out the biblical story with a few extra details, as when he describes Noah's ark as 'shyngled' or clinker-built (IX. 142). This is the same method (though on a very small scale) as that adopted in, for example, the *Gawain*-poet's version of the Jonah story in *Patience*. It observes the principle stated by one medieval French poet, that 'anyone who is speaking truth and according to Holy Scripture ought to follow the letter'.[13] Such literal historical narrative also has its place, of course, within the world of events which Will sees in his dreams; but on that level, in Langland's bold and rapid trajectory from Adam to Friar Penetrans Domos, there is no question of simply 'following the letter' of Scripture. Indeed, what may rather strike one in, for instance, Passus XVIII, is the paucity of literal detail. Someone with no knowledge of the Gospels would find it difficult to reconstruct the course of events in Holy Week from that dream. In this respect, Langland's treatment of the Passion puts him closer to the Anglo-Saxon author of *The Dream of the Rood* than to those of his own contemporaries who gathered all the factual details they could from the four Gospels and amplified them with further details from other sources (as in the mystery cycles). Langland's amplifications are of a different sort, for his are not historical accounts, but what I am calling fictions of history.

Fictions of history are not at all the same thing as historical fictions. Historical novels of the classic kind invest their imagined plots with the same air of reality and truth that attends the historical matrix in which they are set. Sir Walter Scott's Ivanhoe is, or ought to be, as real to the reader of the novel as his Richard the First. But in Langland's poem, as in Spenser's *Faerie Queene*, the process is reversed. Historical persons and events are assimilated into the poetic world of dream or faerie and so lose, in so far as they are distorted or transformed there, their historical character. Not even Langland's Christ should be more real to the reader of the poem than his imagined Piers Plowman—one reason, perhaps, why the work proves capable of appealing as well to unbelievers

---

[13] 'Celui qui verité dit | Et selonc divine escriture | Covient sevre la letreüre', *Le Bestiaire de Gervaise*, ed. Paul Meyer, *Romania*, I (1872), 420–43, lines 24–6.

as to the faithful. Langland shifts the events and persons of salvation-history sideways, as it were, into the parallel world of Will's dreaming. Like Spenser, he shows history at one remove, as if we were seeing its shadow, its outlines through a veil, or its image in a mirror.[14] This is—or was thought to be—the distinctively poetic way of treating history: to shift it into the mode of fiction. Thus, in a note on a line in the first book of Virgil's *Aeneid*, the commentator Servius observes: 'At this point [Virgil] touches *per transitum* upon a historical fact which, according to the law of poetic art, he cannot state openly.'[15] The noun *transitus*, used by Servius here, derives from the verb *transire*, 'to cross over', and it denotes exactly that shift from one mode to another which Langland also effects, the shift into a parallel world of poetic fiction. This is the world in which historical events appear recognizable but transfigured, just as real-life events appear in dreams.

Let us consider first the way Langland introduces real persons from salvation-history into his dream worlds, and how he identifies them there. He is in general good at introducing new characters into his stories—one mark of his strength as a narrative poet. He commonly employs on such occasions what Genette calls the 'topos of novelistic beginning', according to which, when introducing a new character, the author has to pretend not to know him.[16] There are many such intriguing moments in the poem. Piers himself is first introduced as 'a plowman' (V. 537), Thought as 'a muche man, as me thoughte, lik to myselve' (VIII. 71), and Hawkin as 'a mynstral, as me tho thoughte' (XIII. 221). The new figure is presented as he first appears to the dreamer ('as me thoughte'), assigned with an indefinite article to some more or less general class of person: *a* plowman, *a* big man, *a* minstrel. In these particular cases, the effect is straightforward enough, for here fictional characters are in question, as in a novel. But Lang-

[14] On Spenser's terminology, see Michael O'Connor, *Mirror and Veil: The Historical Dimensions of Spenser's Faerie Queene* (Chapel Hill, NC, 1977), 16–17.

[15] Servius on *Aeneid*, I. 382: 'MATRE DEA MONSTRANTE VIAM hoc loco per transitum tangit historiam, quam per legem artis poeticae aperte non potest ponere', *Servianorum in Vergilii Carmina Commentariorum*, Special Publications of the American Philological Association, no. I, ed. E. K. Rand and others, vol. ii (Lancaster, Pa., 1946), 186.

[16] *Narrative Discourse*, 191 n. 53.

land also employs the same topos of novelistic beginning to introduce known scriptural characters into his later dreams, and here the effect is more striking:

> And thanne spak *Spiritus Sanctus* in Gabrielis mouthe
> To a maide that highte Marie, a meke thyng withalle,
> That oon Jesus, a justices sone, moste jouke in hir chambre
> Til *plenitudo temporis* tyme comen were.
>
> (XVI. 90–3)

Spiritus Sanctus, the Holy Spirit, has already figured in the preceding lines, and Gabriel evidently needs no introduction, but Mary and Jesus, strangely enough, do: '*a* maide ... *oon* Jesus'. The indefinite article introducing Mary echoes the text of St Luke's Gospel, where Gabriel is sent 'to a virgin espoused to a man whose name was Joseph, of the house of David: and the virgin's name was Mary' (Luke 1: 27). It is a twice-told tale, which would be told in that form, as if for the first time, whenever Luke's words were read or a preacher wished to evoke the event as a fresh reality rather than as a familiar point of reference in the past. In the world of Will's dream, however, the event is not being narrated; it is—or so we are invited to believe—actually happening before his very eyes; and to that extent (though rather uncertainly here) the indefinite article serves to loosen the moorings attaching the fiction to history. It makes history strange. The effect is more powerful in the following line: 'That oon Jesus, a justices sone, moste jouke in hir chambre'. 'Oon Jesus', 'a certain Jesus': we know which one is meant, of course, but the indefinite formula, together with the strange reference to him as a 'justice's son', effects something of the necessary *transitus*. Similar formulae are used in other cases where scriptural persons first appear. Even the Holy Spirit is introduced, somewhat absurdly, as 'oon *Spiritus Paraclitus*' into Will's vision of Pentecost (XIX. 202). A more successful example is the introduction of Abraham/Faith:

> And thanne mette I with a man, a myd-Lenten Sonday,
> As hoor as an hawethorn, and Abraham he highte.
>
> (XVI. 172–3)

Even better is the introduction of Jesus as he appears for the first time in Will's dream of the Passion: 'Oon semblable to

the Samaritan, and somdeel to Piers the Plowman' (XVIII. 10).
Here, more so than in the earlier 'oon Jesus', the indefiniteness
of the article is exploited to the full. Even though the reader
knows perfectly well that it must be the Jesus who rides into
Jerusalem, it is at the same time, and convincingly, a Jesus
who belongs to the parallel world of dreams.

Another feature of this parallel world is a marked tendency
to avoid calling real persons by their real names. This tend-
ency is apparent already in the first part of the poem. There,
God can be simply 'God' when he is spoken of at the
non-fictional level; but when he figures in the dream world,
albeit off-stage, as the master of Piers's manor or as the giver
of his pardon, he is regularly called 'Truth', just as Satan is
there called 'Wrong'. This device might be described as
personification working in a direction opposite to the normal.
Normal personification takes something that is not a person
at all—reason, mercy, conscience—and fictionalizes it as a
person; but when God appears as 'Truth', it is a real person
that is being, paradoxically, personified and so absorbed into
the fictive world. Thus, in the last part of the poem, the Holy
Spirit, first mysteriously referred to as 'oon *Spiritus Paraclitus*',
is then introduced to the dreamer by Conscience as 'Grace':
'Grace is his name' (XIX. 209); and it is as 'Grace' that he
figures in the ensuing narrative. There are, it is true, special
reasons for veiling divinity in poetic fictions: it is simply
embarrassing when, at the end of the *Songe de Paradis*, the
dreamer enters Paradise and meets God in person.[17] But it is
not only the Godhead that Langland veils in such dream
pseudonyms. He does the same, for instance, with his triad
Abraham, Moses, and the Samaritan.

The introduction of Abraham as 'a man called Abraham'
may seem, despite its curious indefiniteness, to put his identity
beyond doubt; but he introduces himself in different terms:

> 'I am Feith,' quod that freke, 'it falleth noght me to lye,
> And of Abrahames hous an heraud of armes.'
>
> (XVI. 176–7)

It is strange to learn that this 'man called Abraham' is a
herald in Abraham's household, as if he were no more than

---

[17] *Le Songe de Paradis*, ed. Scheler, lines 895 ff.

a proxy or spokesman for the great patriarch, and stranger
still that he should announce himself by a different name
altogether, 'Faith'.[18] Nor are these discrepancies resolved in
what follows. This is and is not Abraham. On the one hand,
he recalls Abraham's encounters with God, reported in Gen-
esis, as his own; Isaac is his son; he has Abraham's 'bosom';
and he is several times simply called 'Abraham'. On the other
hand, he is called 'Faith' equally often, both when he partici-
pates in the story of the Good Samaritan in the role of the
priest who passes by, and also when acting as herald on the
occasion of Christ's entry into Jerusalem. By that time, indeed,
in Passus XVIII, the historical Abraham has been almost
completely dissolved away in the fiction. In the case of Moses,
this process is even more marked. Moses, the second person
in Langland's triad, is in fact never once called by his
historical name: he is always either 'Spes' or 'Hope'. His
opening words clearly identify him with the Old Testament
person:

> 'I am *Spes*, a spie,' quod he, 'and spire after a knyght
> That took me a maundement upon the mount of Synay.'
> (XVII. 1–2)

Yet the text of this 'maundement', as he reveals it written on
a piece of hard rock, proves to be not exactly the Ten
Commandments themselves, but rather a version of Christ's
digest of them (Luke 10: 27); and a later passage suggests that
Hope may not be quite the same as Moses after all:

> Hope cam hippynge after, that hadde so ybosted
> How he with Moyses maundement hadde many men yholpe.
> (XVII. 61–2)

The third member of the triad, the Good Samaritan, is not
a historical person at all, for his origins lie in the imaginary
world of Christ's parable; but he acts as a dream proxy for
Christ himself, and his name provides one of the variety of
designations under which Christ appears in these dreams. On
more than one occasion, it may be remarked, Langland

---

[18] The C Text initially avoids the contradiction by altering Abraham's opening
word to 'I am with fayth' (XVIII. 185), but later simply calls him Fayth (XVIII. 274
etc.).

betrays an interest in the curious fact that one person may bear several names. In Passus XV, observing that the character commonly known as 'Anima' claims to have nine different names, Will jokingly compares him to bishops who have a 'heap' of names: *presul, pontifex, metropolitanus, episcopus,* and *pastor.*[19] On that occasion, Will is reproached for wanting to know 'the cause of all their names'; but, in an extraordinary passage in XIX, having noticed that in the Gospels Christ has several designations, Langland offers to explain their respective 'causes' (XIX. 15–153). Will asks Conscience why he has referred to the son of God as 'Christ', since the Jews called him 'Jesus', and Conscience in reply explains that Jesus was first a knight, then a king, and finally a conqueror. As a knight, in his youth, he was properly called 'Jesus, son of Mary'; then, as king of the Jews, his name was 'Jesus, son of David', marking his royal descent; and as a conqueror, after the Resurrection, he became 'Christ' (a name which the poet perhaps understood to mean 'conqueror'). So the poet has some warrant in Scripture itself for his own multiple naming of Jesus Christ.[20] To these various scriptural names, however, he adds dream designations of his own. Not only does Jesus appear *en travesti* as the Samaritan, but he also acquires, like Abraham and Moses, abstract pseudonyms, as if the second person of the Trinity might equally well be a personification. He can be referred to as 'Truth' and, more frequently, as 'Life':

'Deeth seith he shal fordo and adoun brynge
Al that lyveth or loketh in londe or in watre.
Lif seith that he lieth, and leieth his lif to wedde
That, for al that Deeth kan do, withinne thre daies to walke
And fecche fro the fend Piers fruyt the Plowman.'

(XVIII. 29–33)

---

[19] Compare C XVIII. 192–6, on the 'sondry names' of the members of the Trinity.
[20] This passage may have been suggested by Robert Grosseteste's *Chateau d'Amour.* Citing Isaiah's well-known prophecy (Isa. 9: 6), Grosseteste derives from it six 'names' of Christ (lines 509–18): Wonderful, Counsellor, God, Mighty, Father of the World to Come, and Prince of Peace. He explains the causes of these names by assigning each in turn to a phase of Christ's life, from the Incarnation to the Second Coming (520–1768). Thus, Christ is Mighty at the Harrowing of Hell (1283–1492), Prince of Peace at the Last Judgement (1493–1768): *Le Chateau d'Amour de Robert Grosseteste, évèque de Lincoln,* ed. J. Murray (Paris, 1918).

The foregoing instances, the indefinite introductions and the dream pseudonyms, suggest something of how Langland adapts his historical figures to the fictions in which they play a part. In ways such as these, he assimilates them into his world of dreams. This is a world in which distinctions between fact and fiction, *verité and mençonge*, stand to be overridden.[21] Just as biblical facts can there become fictions, so also biblical fictions can become facts—realities, that is, to the dreaming eye. Medieval commentators on the Bible regularly emphasize (what is in any case obvious) that not all scriptural passages are to be taken literally, as records of historical fact: the authors sometimes speak metaphorically, *per figuras*. But in Langland's imagination the Good Samaritan, the figurative hero of Christ's parable, has the same status as the historical Abraham and Moses with whom he is associated. Similarly, in the vision of the Harrowing of Hell, the approach of Christ towards Hell gate can be observed, not only by the devils who would really have been there, but also by the Four Daughters of God— ladies who belong in the scriptural pre-text, not to history, but to the poetic fancy of the Psalmist, in whose prophetic imaginings 'Mercy and truth have met each other: justice and peace have kissed'. Yet Mercy, Truth, Peace, and Righteousness are just as real, in Will's dream, as Lucifer or Satan.[22]

A less obvious instance of Langland deriving one of his fictions of history from the metaphorical language of the Bible is to be found in his account of the early Church as it was established by Grace, the Holy Spirit. Considered historically, as its context requires, this part of Passus XIX must refer to the period covered by the Acts of the Apostles. Langland directly recalls only one event, the descent of the Holy Spirit, from Acts; but his allegory of the early Church as a farm, in which the seeds of the virtues are cultivated and harvested, has its source in the same book of the Bible. In Acts 17: 18

---

[21] 'The nature of allegory is to integrate fictional and nonfictional discourse', Carolynn Van Dyke, *The Fiction of Truth: Structures of Meaning in Narrative and Dramatic Allegory* (Ithaca, NY, 1985), 44.

[22] By contrast, in his *Chateau d'Amour* Grosseteste clearly distinguishes the fictional status of the Four Daughters story from the historicity of the preceding narrative: 'Ici reposera mun dit; | Si vus dirrai un respit, | Ki bien toche a ma matire' (ed. Murray, lines 201–3). The word *respit*, commonly meaning 'proverb', here evidently denotes a traditional non-literal story or parable.

the Athenian philosophers, speaking better than they knew, refer to St Paul as *seminiverbius*, 'a sower of words'. This expression reminded commentators of Christ's parable of the sower, and also of Paul's own words to the Corinthians: 'I have planted, Apollo watered: but God gave the increase . . . You are God's husbandry' (1 Corinthians 3: 6, 9). Hence there arose a tradition, which Langland follows, of representing the apostolic missions as *Dei agricultura*.[23] The sixth-century poet Arator, whose Latin versification of Acts was a curriculum text in the Middle Ages, uses many images of seedtime and harvest, as in his free version of the apostles' prayer in Acts 4: 24–30: 'Grant that the seeds of the Word [*semina verbi*] may be fostered by your gifts, and that, making use of the fallow land, this company of yours may, with your fructifying help, gather in the sheaves with which you may stock the granaries of your heaven, rewarding the faithful wheat while the tares perish.'[24]

There is much yet to be determined about the scriptural and exegetical sources of Langland's fiction of the apostolic *agricultura*. Thus, it will be unclear to a modern reader why the seeds which Grace, the Holy Spirit, gives Piers to sow in his ploughed field should be identified with the four cardinal virtues, prudence, temperance, fortitude, and justice:

> And Grace gaf Piers greynes—cardynales vertues,
> And sew it in mannes soule, and sithen he tolde hir names.
> *Spiritus Prudencie* the firste seed highte . . .

> (XIX. 276–8)

---

[23] See generally Stephen A. Barney, 'The Plowshare of the Tongue: The Progress of a Symbol from the Bible to *Piers Plowman*', *Mediaeval Studies*, 35 (1973), 261–93.

[24] 'Da semina verbi | Per tua dona coli, signisque novalibus usa | Colligat ista manus te fructificante maniplos | De quibus ipse tui componas horrea caeli | Triticeamque fidem lolio pereunte corones', Arator, *De Actibus Apostolorum*, ed. A. P. McKinley, Corpus Scriptorum Ecclesiasticorum Latinorum 72 (Vienna, 1951), I. 365–9. Compare II. 449–53, on St Paul as *seminiverbius*: 'For he as a fruitful traveller walked and cultivated in the world; and his labour benefitted all, so that God's field might grow, and the purified human mind might bear fruit and not run wild with tares where it ought to bear harvest crops.' See also Arator, I. 54, 518; II. 308–10, 836–44. St Augustine's comment on Paul as 'seminator verborum' and 'messor morum' (*PL* 38.808) was reproduced in the *Glossa Ordinaria* (*PL* 114.460). A Lollard preacher on the parable of the sower speaks of the 'tyme of þe apostlis whiche weren principalli sent of him to sowe þis gostli sed', *Lollard Sermons*, ed. Gloria Cigman, EETS 294 (1989), 100.

It is significant that Langland consistently speaks of the *spirit* of prudence, the *spirit* of temperance, and the rest. This careful form of words shows that he is associating these virtues with the gifts of the Holy Spirit ('Grace') as described by Isaiah in a famous passage of messianic prophecy: 'And there shall come forth a rod out of the root of Jesse: and a flower shall rise up out of his root. And the spirit of the Lord shall rest upon him: the spirit of wisdom and of understanding, the spirit of counsel and of fortitude [*spiritus consilii et fortitudinis*], the spirit of knowledge and of godliness. And he shall be filled with the spirit of the fear of the Lord' (Isaiah 11: 1–3). As Rosemond Tuve has shown, these seven gifts of the Holy Spirit were held to give rise to seven virtues in the soul of man, and these virtues were commonly identified with the four cardinal virtues: 'there is not the slightest hint of rivalry between two sets . . . and the integration, through the use of both sets for definition, defies later separation'.[25] Accordingly, the Middle English *Book of Vices and Virtues* observes: 'Of þe four cardinal vertues speken moch þe olde philosofres, but þe Holy Gost ȝeveþ hem moche bettre and techeþ hem an hundred so wel.'[26] Such, then, are the gifts which Grace grants to the apostolic Church in Langland's poem.

In representing the gifts of the Holy Spirit as seeds or 'greynes', Langland is again following tradition. Hugh of St Victor puts the point exactly: 'The gifts are the first stirrings in the heart—seeds of the virtues, as it were, scattered over the earth of our heart. The virtues themselves grow up like a

---

[25] Rosemond Tuve, *Allegorical Imagery: Some Mediaeval Books and their Posterity* (Princeton, NJ, 1966), 88. The whole of Tuve's ch. 2 is relevant. R. W. Frank, *Piers Plowman and the Scheme of Salvation* (New Haven, Conn., 1957), in a valuable discussion on pp. 104–5, cites St Gregory on the gift of the Spirit 'which, in the mind It works on, forms first of all Prudence, Temperance, Fortitude, Justice': see *Moralia in Job*, ed. M. Adriaen, Corpus Christianorum: Series Latina 143 (Turnholt, 1979), Bk. II, ch. 49, lines 37–9. It may be noted that, as well as deriving '*Spiritus Fortitudinis*' from Isaiah's list, Langland also refers later (albeit ironically) to '*Spiritus Intellectus*', the second of Isaiah's gifts: B XIX. 466.

[26] *The Book of Vices and Virtues*, ed. W. Nelson Francis, EETS 217 (1942), 122, cited by Frank, *Scheme of Salvation*, 104, and by Morton W. Bloomfield, *Piers Plowman as a Fourteenth-Century Apocalypse* (New Brunswick, NJ, n.d. [1961]), n. 30 to p. 134. Bloomfield's discussion is valuable, but he fails to note the crucial passage from Isaiah.

crop from these.'[27] The distinction between the gifts and the
virtues to which they give rise, here touched upon by Hugh,
is treated with scholastic precision by Thomas Aquinas in his
*Summa Theologica*;[28] but Langland handles the matter allegori-
cally. The seeds *Spiritus Prudencie* and the rest, representing the
first impulses towards virtue inspired by Grace, grow up and
yield the harvest which Piers gathers into the barn of the
Church, Unity. Piers thus stocks the church with good men
and women. However, the growth of the virtues out of the
gift-seeds is essentially an internal spiritual process; so Lang-
land also, at some cost to the coherence of his fiction, insists
that the seeds themselves are to be eaten. So,

> *Spiritus Prudencie* the firste seed highte;
> And whoso ete that, ymagynen he sholde,
> Er he dide any dede, devyse wel the ende.[29]

Thus we are to imagine the prudential virtue of foresight and
all the rest growing up like a plant inside the person within
whom the Holy Ghost first inspires them.[30]

Not all Langland's fictions of history have scriptural or
exegetical sources, however. In particular, once the apostolic
barn of the church is converted, somewhat awkwardly, into a
'peel' or fortified farmstead (XIX. 366) to be defended against
Pride and the Antichrist, the allegory takes on a distinctively
medieval character. Langland's handling of the siege narrative
with which his poem ends is a little slapdash, perhaps showing
a decline in his taste or capacity for story-telling. The attack
by Kind is very well done, but Antichrist and his army of sins
are sketchy and unconvincing.[31] The best episode is the last,

---

[27] 'Dona sunt primi motus in corde, quasi quaedam semina virtutum jactata super
terram cordis nostri; virtutes quasi seges quae ex ipsis consurgunt', Hugh of St Victor,
*Summa Sententiarum*, Tract. III, cap. xvii (*PL* 176.114). Compare the passage from Arator
cited above (n. 24), where the seeds of the Word are fostered by the Gifts.

[28] *Summa Theologica*, 1–2 q.68 a.1, 'Utrum dona differant a virtutibus'.

[29] B XIX. 278–80. See also lines 284, 292, and 300.

[30] A passage in B XII, lines 59–63, revised as C XIV. 23–7, treats the mysterious
relationship between grace and good works with some rather similar plant imagery.
Thus, God 'sent forth the seynt espirit to do love sprynge' (C XIV. 27).

[31] Thomas Warton long ago suggested that Langland 'here had his eye on the old
French *Roman d'Antechrist*, a poem written by Huon de Meri, about the year 1228'
(*History of English Poetry*, ed. cit. ii. 121). This is likely enough. *Li Tornoiemenz Antecrit*
was an influential allegorical poem: see Marc-René Jung, *Études sur le poème allégorique*

where with typical ingenuity the poet adapts St Paul's prophe-
cy of the last days to the circumstances of his siege story.[32]
The hypocrite who 'creeps into houses' here, in the person of
Friar Flatterer, Sir Penetrans Domos, gains entrance to the
embattled stronghold by guile and 'enchants' the garrison with
his physic. In contrast to the preceding direct assault by the
sins, this sinister little episode of infiltration perfectly embodies
Langland's fears for the modern Church, threatened not by
identifiable dangers of persecution or heresy, but by the
insidious workings of hypocrisy. It is like the moment in the
*Psychomachia* of Prudentius, where the direct confrontation
between virtues and vices has a treacherous aftermath: when
the battle is over, Discordia enters the holy city in disguise
and stabs Concordia.[33]

Langland devotes more care to his earlier allegory of the
Christ-knight's joust with Satan and his victory over the
powers of Hell. The sheer narrative power of this section
resides chiefly in the sense of excited anticipation that it
conveys, first on the road to Jerusalem and then in the
darkness of Hell. On the road, Abraham, Moses, and the
Samaritan hurry towards Jerusalem for the great joust; and
in Hell, the devils and the Four Daughters of God watch in
fear or wonder the approach of the Christ of the Harrowing.
Less obvious, perhaps, is the ingenuity and wit with which

---

*en France au Moyen Age* (Berne, 1971), 268–89. Georg Wimmer, in his edition of the
*Tornoiemenz* (Marburg, 1888), identifies two of the seven manuscript copies known to
him as of English provenance. The fighting around Langland's besieged 'peel'
between the forces of Antichrist and Conscience bears only a general resemblance to
Huon's tournament; but the involvement of Huon's narrator in the action may well
have suggested the similar involvement of Will (XX. 183–213), as Dorothy L. Owen
proposed: *Piers Plowman: A Comparison with some Earlier and Contemporary French Allegories*
(London, 1912; reprinted 1978), 82, 148. Like Will, Huon gets caught up in the
fighting, accidentally struck to the heart by one of Venus's arrows (lines 2582–754).
After the tournament is over, the wounded Huon is directed by Contrition to
Confession and at last enters the city Esperance (which corresponds to Langland's
barn Unity): 'Devocion | Me mena a Confession | Et Penitance la miresse. | Parmi
une sauchoie espesse | M'en ving tot droit a Esperance' (3099–103). Compare *Piers*:
'I comsed to rome | Thorugh Contricion and Confession til I cam to Unitee' (XX.
212–13).

[32] See n. 4 above.

[33] *Psychomachia*, lines 667 ff., in *Prudentius*, ed. and trans. H. J. Thomason, Loeb
edn., vol. i (Cambridge, Mass., 1949). The similarity is noted by Stephen A. Barney,
*Allegories of History, Allegories of Love* (Hamden, Conn., 1979), 94.

Langland shifts Christ's life into a chivalric mode. It is likely that he had read Deguileville's *Pelerinage de Jhesucrist*, in which his French predecessor allegorized Christ's life as a pilgrimage.[34] Narratives of this kind require of the author a sustained act of improvisation. Sometimes an actual event can be incorporated as it stands into the fiction. Thus Deguileville can represent the infant Christ's journey into Egypt as the first leg of his pilgrimage on earth.[35] Similarly, the actual piercing of Christ's side by Longeus' spear on the cross fits easily into Langland's story of the jousting. More often, however, it is a question of drawing remoter analogies between the historical tenor and the allegorical vehicle, and shaping the fiction accordingly. So Deguileville's pilgrim Christ rests for nine months in Mary's chamber as his 'premiere station', before setting out on his journey.[36] At their worst, such analogies can be very strained, as when Deguileville observes that Jesus suffered Judas to kiss him because pilgrims are accustomed to be kissed by all and sundry.[37]

Langland was by no means the first to treat Christ as a knight; and several of the possible analogies had already been exploited by earlier writers.[38] A particularly striking case is the analogy between the Incarnation and knightly incognito: just as a great knight might adopt the arms of some lesser man in order that his reputation should not deter opponents from encountering him at a tourney, so Christ adopted humanity in preparation for his encounter with Satan. Exactly this idea is to be found in an earlier Anglo-Norman allegory, where the Christ-knight 'takes the arms of a bachelor of his called Adam', because his enemy, Belial, would never have dared to

[34] See further Appendix A.

[35] *Pelerinage de Jhesucrist*, line 3573, refers to the Jesus of the flight into Egypt as 'le petit pelerin'.

[36] 'C'est la premiere station | De ta peregrination', *Jhesucrist*, lines 1293–4.

[37] 'Bien ont pieca acoustumé | Pelerins que on les baise, | Non obstant que pou leur plaise', *Jhesucrist*, lines 8288–90.

[38] See Wilbur Gaffney, 'The Allegory of the Christ-Knight in *Piers Plowman*', *PMLA* 46 (1931), 155–68; Raymond Saint-Jacques, 'Langland's Christ-Knight and the Liturgy', *Revue de l'Université d'Ottawa*, 37 (1967), 146–58; J. A. W. Bennett, *Poetry of the Passion* (Oxford, 1982), 99–112; R. A. Waldron, 'Langland's Originality: The Christ-Knight and the Harrowing of Hell', in Gregory Kratzmann and James Simpson (eds.), *Medieval English Religious and Ethical Literature: Essays in Honour of G. H. Russell* (Cambridge, 1986), 66–81.

encounter him if he knew his true identity.[39] In the same way, Faith, in his role of herald, identifies Langland's incognito knight in the Palm Sunday episode as Jesus, but Jesus wearing the arms of human nature in order that his divinity should neither be recognized nor suffer injury (XVIII. 22–6). Langland elaborates upon this idea, however, by attributing these arms to Piers the Plowman:

> 'This Jesus of his gentries wol juste in Piers armes,
> In his helm and in his haubergeon—*humana natura*.'
> (XVIII. 22–3)

There is a price to be paid for thus introducing the Plowman into the chivalric fiction. Piers is not accidentally or casually a plowman. His occupation to a large extent defines what he stands for in the poem. To change his occupation is therefore to attack the very core of his meaning; yet that is what Langland does here—for a plowman, as Dr Johnson might have said, has no armour to lend. The new casting is otherwise well handled, however. Langland has reimagined Piers as one of those older knights who, in reality as in romance, took young ones under their wing and acted as their patron and helper. In the French life of William the Marshal, for instance, William acts as 'mestre' to the Young King Henry—'sire e mestre de son seignor'—and also, as a very old man, to the child Henry III.[40] And in Langland's own lifetime, Simon Burley acted as 'mestre' to the young Richard II.[41] Such is exactly the part that Piers plays, earlier in the B Text, in relation to the youthful Jesus of Passus XVI. The divine child is there described as so supremely promising, so richly endowed with knightly spirit, that he wishes to fight his great battle before the time is ripe, 'er ful tyme come'. But—

---

[39] Nicholas Bozon, *Du roi ki avait une amye*, ed. T. Wright, in *The Chronicle of Pierre de Langtoft*, vol. ii, Rolls Series (London, 1868), 426, lines 17–24. For a romance parallel, compare Lancelot borrowing Tirry's shield in order to ride to the tournament disguised, in Malory, *Works*, 3rd edn., ed. E. Vinaver, rev. P. J. C. Field (Oxford, 1990), 1067: 'lende me a shylde that were nat opynly knowyn, for myne ys well knowyn'.

[40] *L'Histoire de Guillaume le Maréchal*, ed. P. Meyer (Paris, 1891–1901), lines 1966, 2634, 3654; 15590, 18006.

[41] See Nicholas Orme, *From Childhood to Chivalry: The Education of the English Kings and Aristocracy*, 1066–1530 (London, 1984), 18–21, 24–5, 82–3, 227.

> Piers the Plowman parceyved plener tyme,
> And lered hym lechecraft, his lif for to save,
> That though he were wounded with his enemy,
>    to warisshen hymselve;
> And dide hym assaie his surgenrie on hem that sike were,
> Til he was parfit praktisour, if any peril fille.
>
>                 (XVI. 103–7)

This is a brilliant example of *mençonge* expressing a *verité*. A chivalric 'mestre' may well be intrinsically inferior to his charge, as is the young Perceval's master, Gornemans; yet he will have more knowledge and experience of life. So Piers, though not himself divine, can teach the young Jesus to bide his time, and also instruct him in the knightly arts of surgery.[42] The theological meaning of this is that God—even God—had to learn what it was to be human, and submit to the conditions and restraints of that inferior state.[43] Among other things, this explains the curious fact that Jesus began his ministry so late in life, after living in private (under tuition, as it were) for thirty long years.

    The introduction of Piers Plowman into Langland's version of salvation-history, here and elsewhere, is surely one of his boldest strokes—a truly audacious combining of fiction with fact, which must qualify him to count among Harold Bloom's 'strong poets' along with Dante, Milton, and Blake.[44] Most of his other imaginary intruders into history—the Good Samaritan, the Daughters of God, the Sins—are traditional figures, but Piers is a creation of his own. What is more, the poet

---

[42] See the treatment of Christ's knightly *enfance* in Michelle Martindale, 'The Treatment of the Life of Christ in *Piers Plowman*', B.Litt. thesis (Oxford, 1978). Martindale notes that medical skill was a recognized knightly accomplishment (pp. 53–4). See, for instance, *Guillaume le Maréchal*, ed. cit., lines 1789–92, where the marshal is said to excel both 'Ypocras' and 'Galiens' as a surgeon.

[43] This interpretation was proposed by David Aers, *Piers Plowman and Christian Allegory* (London, 1975), 107–9, and also, independently, by Daniel M. Murtaugh, *'Piers Plowman' and the Image of God* (Gainesville, Fla., 1978), 119–21. See also Samuel A. Overstreet, 'Langland's Elusive Plowman', *Traditio*, 45 (1989–90), 257–341; 309–14. The idea that God had something to learn about what it was to be human (Murtaugh cites Luke 2: 52 and Heb. 5: 8) finds expression also at B XIX. 96–101 and especially C XX. 217–18. On his desire to learn, see B XVI. 215 and XVIII. 213, 221–4. For a Deguileville parallel, see Appendix A, p. 117 below.

[44] Harold Bloom, *Ruin the Sacred Truths: Poetry and Belief from the Bible to the Present* (Cambridge, Mass., 1989).

represents his creation as playing, in the history of mankind, a distinctly more essential role than any of the other fictions. He is a decisive presence in Old and New Testament times, and a decisive absence in Langland's own day. The general idea seems clear enough, to show the positive role played by human nature at its inspired best in the history of man's salvation; but the imaginative rendering of that idea is anything but commonplace.

The outcome is two triumphs and one disaster. The disaster comes first, in the Tree of Charity episode at the beginning of the historical sequence. Piers, it will be recalled, is here cast as the master of the garden in which the tree grows. At the first conversion of that tree from the moral to the historical, when its fruit comes to be seen as the worthies of the Old Testament, this piece of casting continues to make sense—their virtue being fostered by that potentiality in human nature which Piers represents. But then, for once, the poet's lively narrative imagination leads him astray. Picturing the devil as a scrumper or apple-stealer, and Piers as an angry gardener defending his crop from the raid, Langland has Piers 'for pure tene' strike out at the robber with one of the three poles or props by which the tree is supported. This would be all very well if that pole were not a member of the Trinity, God the Son. The event being represented, in fact, is the Incarnation, as the immediately following vision of the Annunciation makes clear. Yet nothing that Piers represents, I believe, can possibly be supposed to have initiated the Incarnation. Langland evidently came later to recognize that things had gone wrong in this passage; for in the C Text he writes Piers out of the episode altogether and substitutes for him at the crucial point *Libera-Voluntas-Dei*, the free will of God. This makes easy theological sense: God of his own free will sent his son to earth. It also illustrates Langland's tendency, in the C revision, to treat his earlier imaginings rather ruthlessly, as if they no longer held his interest; but in this particular case something surely had to be done to clear up the mess.

In what follows, as we have noted, Piers is associated with the human nature of Christ. Here the allegory works particularly well. The casting of Piers in the role of chivalric 'mestre' succeeds both intellectually and imaginatively. Langland

manages to suggest thoughts about the relationship of divinity
to humanity in the person of Christ which could perhaps
hardly be expressed in scholastic prose; and in the process he
achieves two moments of authentic visionary intensity and
strangeness. The first, as all readers agree, is the moment
when the Christ of the Entry into Jerusalem is seen as 'oon
semblable to the Samaritan, and somdeel to Piers the Plow-
man'. The second occurs at the beginning of the follow-
ing dream. In the course of his Easter morning mass, Will
falls asleep:

> and sodeynly me mette
> That Piers the Plowman was peynted al blody,
> And com in with a cros bifore the comune peple,
> And right lik in alle lymes to oure lord Jesu.
> And thanne called I Conscience to kenne me the sothe:
> 'Is this Jesus the justere,' quod I, 'that Jewes dide to dethe?
> Or it is Piers the Plowman! Who peynted hym so rede?'
> Quod Conscience, and kneled tho, 'Thise arn Piers armes—
> Hise colours and his cote armure; ac he that cometh so blody
> Is Crist with his cros, conquerour of Cristene.'
>
> (XIX. 5-14)

This extraordinary vision—I hesitate to call it a fiction—is
based on another figurative passage of Scripture, in Isaiah 63:
'Who is this that cometh from Edom, with dyed garments
from Bosra, this beautiful one in his robe, walking in the
greatness of his strength? I, that speak justice and am a
defender to save. Why then is thy apparel red, and thy
garments like theirs that tread in the winepress?' (Isaiah 63:
1-2). The poet applies this vision, commonly taken as Issiah's
prophecy of Christ, to the Christ of the Resurrection. In the
process, he adapts its question-and-answer form to the cir-
cumstances of the dream.[45] Will questions Conscience ('Who

---

[45] The title 'Christ', according to what Conscience goes on to explain, evidently
identifies this visionary figure as the Resurrected Lord, *Christus resurgens*, the conqueror
of sin and death (B XIX. 62-3, 152, 160). So J. A. W. Bennett, *Poetry of the Passion*,
77. Martindale, 'Treatment of the Life of Christ', 161-8, discusses the passage at
length, citing Jerome's Commentary on Isaiah. Jerome interprets the dialogue as
taking place between wondering angels in heaven ('Who is this that cometh from
Edom?') and the triumphant Christ ('I, that speak justice'), either after the Harrowing
of Hell when he conducts rescued souls to their reward, or else at his own Ascension.

is this that cometh?'), just as he earlier questioned Faith about
his Palm Sunday vision. In each case the uncertainty, attend-
ing the identity of so many figures in this part of the poem,
serves to convey a theological mystery, that of the 'god-man',
one person with two natures.

What follows, though less vivid, is equally well contrived.
The name Piers is a familiar form of Peter, and an association
between the imaginary Piers and the historical St Peter has
been present as a possibility ever since Piers first entered the
poem with the apostle's name on his lips: ' "Peter!" quod a
plowman, and putte forth his hed' (v. 537).[46] Yet it must come
as a surprise that Conscience, in his narrative of the post-
Resurrection appearances of Christ, should be able to slip so
easily from speaking of St Peter to speaking of Piers, as if the
interchangeability of the two names required no explanation
or excuse. Conscience describes how 'Peter' visits the empty
sepulchre (XIX. 163, John 20: 2–9), and how it is 'to Peter and
to hise apostles' that Christ appears in the episode of Doubting
Thomas (XIX. 169, John 20: 26–9); but then—

> 'whan this dede was doon, Dobest he thoughte,
> And yaf Piers power, and pardon he grauntede:
> To alle maner men, mercy and foryifnesse;
> To hym, myghte men to assoille of alle manere synnes,
> In covenaunt that thei come and kneweliche to paye
> To Piers pardon the Plowman—*Redde quod debes.*
> Thus hath Piers power, be his pardon paied,
> To bynde and unbynde bothe here and ellis,
> And assoille men of alle synnes save of dette one.'
>                                        (XIX. 183–91)

Conscience here refers to Christ's appearance to Peter and
other disciples in Galilee at the sea of Tiberias—the episode
which, as recorded by St John in the last chapter of his gospel,
immediately follows the episode of Doubting Thomas, as it
does in the poem. Langland's version, however, also recalls

---

Martindale understands Langland to have had the former occasion in mind. But in
his fiction, where the questions are asked by Will, the occasion can be a post-
Resurrection appearance, as the narrative order of the visions requires.

[46] For further discussion of the relationship between Piers and St Peter, see
Appendix B.

an earlier Petrine passage, for it replaces Christ's parting
charge to Peter in Galilee, 'feed my sheep' (John 21: 15–17),
with one based on Christ's much earlier promise to him: 'thou
art Peter, and upon this rock I will build my church. And the
gates of hell shall not prevail against it. And I will give to
thee the keys of the kingdom of heaven. And whatsoever thou
shalt bind upon earth, it shall be bound also in heaven: and
whatsoever thou shalt loose on earth, it shall be loosed also
in heaven' (Matthew 16: 18–19).[47] This famous passage (the
foundation of later claims for the papacy) leads naturally on
to what follows in the poem. Piers is now seen to represent,
in his last manifestation, the power of human nature under
grace, as it was exerted by the first leader of the Church, and
as it might still be exerted by his papal successors if only they
were worthy to do so.

After Conscience has finished speaking, and as if in confir-
mation of his words, Will himself sees his visionary hero in
the role of St Peter at Pentecost:

> and thanne cam, me thoughte,
> Oon *Spiritus Paraclitus* to Piers and to hise felawes.
>                                          (XIX. 201–2)

In what follows, Piers continues to play the same part, as
leader of the apostolic Church—until, that is, his sudden and
unheralded departure. This departure evidently takes place at
the moment when Grace, having established the sacraments,
sets off 'as wide as the world is, with Piers to tilie truthe' (XIX.
335). From this point on, Piers is no longer spoken of as a
presence in the barn Unity; and his absence is confirmed at
the very end of the poem, when Conscience determines to
become a pilgrim 'and walken as wide as the world lasteth,
| To seken Piers the Plowman, that Pryde myghte destruye'
(XX. 382–3).

---

[47] The same promise about binding and loosing is recorded at Matt. 18: 18. It is
there addressed to the disciples generally, not specifically to St Peter; but it is Peter
who on that occasion goes on to ask the question about forgiveness; and to this Christ
replies with the very parable from which Langland takes the motto of Piers's pardon:
*redde quod debes*, 'pay what thou owest' (Matt. 18: 28). It would seem that this passage,
as well as that in Matt. 16, was associated in the poet's mind with the charge in
John 21.

There is evidence here, as elsewhere, of Langland's close acquaintance with the Acts of the Apostles. In Will's dream, the departure of Piers represents the transition between the charismatic apostolic Church and its unworthy modern successor. It is a mysterious moment, unmarked by specific historical reference to any one of those events which were commonly held to have marked the decline of the Church into worldliness.[48] Yet Langland's fiction has, I suggest, its inspiration in biblical history. It is surely no coincidence that St Peter, after playing such a prominent part in the first half of Acts, should disappear from the rest of the book just as mysteriously as Piers does in the poem. As one biblical scholar says of Peter, the apostle strangely 'vanishes completely from the narrative' after Acts Chapter 15.[49] Noteworthy, too, is the same scholar's observation that the vanishing of Peter marks 'his final transfer to exclusively missionary activity', and testifies to his distinctively 'universalistic point of view';[50] for such a missionary and universalistic role matches exactly what we are able to gather of the absent Piers in the last part of Langland's poem. Piers departs with Grace to till truth 'as wide as the world is', and he is to be sought by Conscience 'as wide as the world lasteth'—expressions which suggest maximal extension in both time and space.[51] The same universalistic note is struck by the 'lewed vicar', when he expresses the wish that Piers might one day be 'emperour of al the world—that all men were Cristene' (XIX. 430). The wish is also the poet's. Like Robert Grosseteste and many others, Langland found it hard to understand why the Christian Church, which had grown to embrace so large a portion of

[48] One such event was the Donation of Constantine, referred to elsewhere, B XV. 555–67.

[49] Oscar Cullmann, *Peter: Disciple–Apostle–Martyr*, trans. Floyd V. Filson (London, 1953), 39. On the same page Cullmann also remarks that Acts 12: 17, 'And going out, he went into another place', serves to indicate 'a transition in the activity of Peter and also in his position in the Primitive Church'.

[50] Ibid. 22, 41–2, and see 65–6. For the 'universalism' of Peter, see Acts 2: 39, 10: 28, 10: 34–6, 11: 5–18, 15: 7–11.

[51] In a passage added in the C Text, expressing the hope that 'alle landes loveden and in on lawe bilevede', Langland uses similar language: churchmen should 'wende as wyde as þe worlde were | To tulie þe erthe with tonge and teche men to lovye' (C x. 198–9).

the known world under Peter and his small band of fellow-workers, should now prove incapable, with all its mighty apparatus, of completing the mission.[52] Something is evidently missing, and that something he embodies in his imaginary avatar of St Peter, Piers the Plowman.

Fictions of history can serve a variety of purposes. Where contemporary affairs are in question, one intention may be to defamiliarize familiar situations by shifting them sideways into a parallel world of the imagination, thus offering them for fresh appraisal (as in *Faerie Queene* Book V) or for satirical contemplation (as in Dryden's *Absalom and Achitophel* or Orwell's *Animal Farm*). Langland, however, rarely touches upon current events in this fashion.[53] His fictions of history are predominantly concerned with sacred history; and the prime effect of these, in his poem, is to bring biblical events to bear upon the moral and spiritual life of a modern individual, Long Will. Thus, his use of abstract pseudonyms for historical individuals identifies in their actions a universal and timeless application: it is as 'Faith' that the patriarch Abraham bears upon life in contemporary Cornhill. Similarly, it is as the imaginary Piers that the Apostle Peter can represent an as yet unrealized potentiality in the fourteenth-century Church. For purposes such as these, the dream form has a peculiar aptness. When past events (whether from our own experience or not) furnish the material for a dream, we cannot be said merely to recall them. Rather, so far as subjective experience is concerned, they could be said to happen all over again. In that sense, an event such as the Harrowing of Hell, when Will witnesses it in his dream, may be said to be happening again for his benefit, albeit 'not really'. The experience is one not just of recollection but of re-enactment—a making present of past events.

In this respect dream functions much like liturgy; for in the *anamnesis* of liturgical celebration the Church at large re-enacts each year the sequence of salvation-history. In the action of the liturgy, as in dream, a biblical event may be said to

[52] See R. W. Southern, *Robert Grosseteste* (Oxford, 1986), 278; and compare B XV. 436–40, 490–530, 603–10,

[53] Examples may be found in the fable of the belling of the cat in the Prologue, and in the debate between Conscience and Lady Meed in Passus III.

happen 'this very night', *hac nocte*. So it is appropriate that the course of biblical events in Will's dreams should run parallel, sporadically at least, with the re-enactment of those events in the liturgical year. In Passus XVIII, most notably, Will falls asleep on Palm Sunday to dream of the Entry into Jerusalem, and is woken from dreaming of the Harrowing of Hell by the clamour of Easter bells. Furthermore, this dream itself blends liturgical with scriptural matter: the antiphonal singing of Palm Sunday in lines 7–8, and the Easter *Te Deum* at line 424.[54] So biblical events figure as living contemporary realities both for the dreaming Will and also for the liturgical community to which he belonged.[55]

Langland was a poet as well as a Christian, and his dream versions of biblical events also gave him a wonderful freedom to exercise his imagination within the story-space of his poem. No paraphrasing version of the Bible, however richly executed (as by the *Gawain*-poet in *Patience*), could have afforded him the freedom to imagine Abraham, Moses, and the Samaritan as a triad representing faith, hope, and charity, or to blend his own imagined Piers with the apostle Peter. Langland accordingly might have read with some satisfaction what the standard encyclopaedia of his day, Isidore of Seville's *Etymologiae*, had to say about the distinction between a poet and a historian: 'The business of the poet is to transform events that have really happened and make them look different by employing, with a certain beauty and grace, figurative devices which refer to them obliquely [*obliquis figurationibus*]. That is why Lucan is not counted among the poets, for he seems to have written histories, not a poem.'[56]

---

[54] See Bruce Harbert, 'Langland's Easter', in Helen Phillips (ed.), *Langland, the Mystics and the Medieval English Religious Tradition: Essays in Honour of S. S. Hussey* (Cambridge, 1990), 57–70. Similarly, the Pentecost hymn *Veni Creator Spiritus* expresses Will's response in his vision of that event (XIX. 211–12).

[55] See M. F. Vaughan, 'The Liturgical Perspectives of *Piers Plowman* B XVI–XIX', *Studies in Medieval and Renaissance History*, 3 (1980), 87–155, especially on the 'moral and present-oriented modality' of liturgical *anamnesis* (p. 106).

[56] 'Officium autem poetae in eo est ut ea, quae vere gesta sunt, in alias species obliquis figurationibus cum decore aliquo conversa transducant. Unde et Lucanus ideo in numero poetarum non ponitur, quia videtur historias conposuisse, non poema', *Etymologiae*, ed. Lindsay, VIII. 7, 10. Isidore refers to Lucan's poem on the civil war in Rome, the *Pharsalia*.

# CHAPTER 4

# Fictions of Self?

The discussion so far has treated fiction as if it were an unproblematic category. Thus, in talking about fictions of history, I made a simple distinction between *verité* and *mençonge*. From a modern point of view, certainly, the distinction between history and fiction could not be so sharply or so simply drawn. Hayden White has argued that every historical narrative, by virtue of being 'emplotted', will be assimilated to the common patterns of all story-telling, fact or fiction; and to that rule the history of salvation, as Langland reflects it, is no exception. To adopt for a moment the terminology borrowed by White from Northrop Frye: salvation-history follows first the pattern of Romance, showing a series of forerunners culminating in the supreme triumph of a hero over his adversaries. It then shifts into the Ironic mode, as the hero's triumph is followed by a disappointing, unheroic aftermath.[1] This is obviously not a series of unconnected historical particulars, but a story with a shape; and as such, it can provide a shape for the third and last part of Langland's poem. What is more, by virtue of its downbeat conclusion, it matches the shape of the two imaginary master-plots that precede it, both of which end in uncertainty and suspense—the struggle for social reform in Passus I–VII, and Will's search for Dowel in Passus VIII–XIII. So fictional and historical stories can live happily side by side in the poem's dream worlds. Yet the fact remains that the distinction between the two, if it is considered historically, emerges clearly enough. Langland and his readers would certainly, if challenged, have been able to say what in the poem was biblical *verité* and what poetic *mençonge*; and we are able to know what they would have said. The Good Samaritan and Piers the Plowman belong to fiction, Abraham and Peter to history.

[1] Hayden White, *Metahistory: The Historical Imagination in Nineteenth-Century Europe* (Baltimore and London, 1973), 7–11, 231–3.

The subject of the present chapter, however, is 'fictions of self', and here matters cannot be so simple. For one thing, the self in question belongs to an author about whom almost nothing is known beyond what he himself may have conveyed to us in his poem. So how, in the absence of external evidence, is one to set about distinguishing autobiographical fact from dream fiction? Professor George Kane has established beyond all reasonable doubt that the first-person narrator, the dreamer Will, bears the poet's own baptismal name, and would have been understood to do so by readers acquainted with the conventions of dream poetry.[2] To that extent— nominally—Will is William Langland, just as Geoffrey in the *House of Fame* is Geoffrey Chaucer. This is by no means an insignificant fact; yet it is hard to know what further inferences it warrants. For one thing, like William Shakespeare in his Sonnets, Langland evidently took advantage of the fact that his name coincided, in its familiar form, with the common noun 'will'. So Will the dreamer represents, to an indeterminable degree, not an individual William but a universal human attribute. He is a personification as well as a person.

The question of so-called 'autobiographical elements' in *Piers Plowman* has prompted a certain amount of disagreement and controversy over the years. Discussion has mainly concerned those particular, individualizing facts about Long Will that the poem offers from time to time: he is tall, he lives in Cornhill with his wife Kit and a daughter Calote, and he earns an uncertain living by praying for his benefactors. The poem's great Victorian editor, W. W. Skeat, took all these things at face value and constructed from them 'the author's life'.[3] Very few modern readers would go so far; indeed, contemporary opinion inclines, on the whole, towards doubt or disbelief. Thus Professor Kane, in an influential lecture

[2] George Kane, *Piers Plowman: The Evidence for Authorship* (London, 1965), ch. 4, 'Signatures'. For an elaborate discussion of Langland's 'signatures' as they develop in the three versions of the poem, see Anne Middleton, 'William Langland's "Kynde Name": Authorial Signature and Social Identity in Late Fourteenth-Century England', in Lee Patterson (ed.), *Literary Practice and Social Change in Britain, 1380–1530* (Berkeley, Calif., 1990), 15–82.

[3] W. W. Skeat (ed.), *The Vision of William Concerning Piers the Plowman in Three Parallel Texts*, 2 vols. (Oxford, 1886), ii, pp. xxxii–xxxviii.

entitled 'The Autobiographical Fallacy in Chaucer and Langland Studies', has argued forcefully in favour of an agnostic suspension of judgement in this matter. Scholarship, he concludes, is 'obliged, in the face of tantalizing biographical possibilities, to acknowledge that we cannot, and strictly speaking should not try to, establish these'.[4] Thus, there is only one fact about Long Will, apart from his baptismal name, that is certainly also a fact about his creator. The dreamer is not only a dreamer; he is also a maker, a poet, and his 'making' is the poem *Piers Plowman* itself.[5] But the fact that William Langland wrote *Piers Plowman* is the only thing we know for sure about him. There is no such external evidence as we have from documents in the case of Thomas Hoccleve, for instance.[6] Hoccleve speaks in his poems of his work and his colleagues in the Office of the Privy Seal, and official records authenticate many of the details; but there are no documents (what documents would there be?) to prove that Langland lived in a cottage on Cornhill with his wife and daughter. He either did or he did not; but we cannot expect to know which.

It therefore seems eminently sensible to suggest, as does Kane, that we should simply suspend judgement on such matters. In practice, however, suspending judgement proves to be a difficult operation, alike for readers and for scholars. The difficulty is to keep the judgement suspended vertically, as it were, without inclining towards either belief on the one side or disbelief on the other. Indeed, my experience suggests that it is actually impossible to avoid betraying an inclination

[4] 'The Autobiographical Fallacy in Chaucer and Langland Studies', the R. W. Chambers Memorial Lecture for 1965, reprinted in Kane, *Chaucer and Langland: Historical and Textual Approaches* (London, 1989), 1–14; 14.

[5] On the representation of Long Will as a writer, see Kane, *Evidence for Authorship*, 62–4, and n. 30 below. It may be noted here that Will's presence on the Malvern Hills (Prol. 5, VII. 142) is consistent with the evidence that Langland himself was brought up in South-West Worcestershire: see M. L. Samuels, 'Langland's Dialect', *Medium Aevum*, 54 (1985), 232–47, reprinted in J. J. Smith (ed.), *The English of Chaucer and his Contemporaries* (Aberdeen, 1988), 70–85.

[6] For some of the Hoccleve documents, see F. J. Furnivall and I. Gollancz (eds.), *Hoccleve's Works: The Minor Poems*, EETS ES 61, 73, rev. Jerome Mitchell and A. I. Doyle, reprinted in one vol. (1970), pp. li–lxxii. Discussion by J. A. Burrow, 'Autobiographical Poetry in the Middle Ages: The Case of Thomas Hoccleve', in J. A. Burrow (ed.), *Middle English Literature: British Academy Gollancz Lectures* (Oxford, 1989), 223–46.

in one or other direction; and if this is so, the matter can hardly be laid to rest on Kane's terms. Strictly speaking, as Kane shows, we can never know; but in practice, everyone leans one way or the other. Thus, recent academic criticism has, for a variety of reasons, inclined towards disbelief, stressing the conventionally fictive character of such 'autobiographical' particulars (and regularly guarding the word 'autobiographical' between inverted commas). Kane's own arguments have been taken to justify that leaning; and his scrupulous agnosticism has been invoked in the cause of something more like atheism. Such criticism prefers to treat Long Will as an imaginary persona—as if the poet himself might well, for all we know, have been a short fat man living in Westminster.

Although, in the absence of external evidence, there can be no decisive solution to such a problem, considerations of literary history will have some bearing upon it. The problem, it should be noted, is by no means peculiar to *Piers Plowman*. On the contrary, in writings of a religious, moral, or satirical kind, later medieval writers quite commonly offer the reader what purport to be particulars about themselves. Thus, the thirteenth-century French poet Rutebeuf complains that, on top of his recent unhappy marriage, he has now lost the sight of his right eye, which was his best eye.[7] In a modern novel this would no doubt pass for one of those unmotivated details which there commonly contribute to the naturalistic effect— the illusion, that is, of things as they just happen to be. But older authors do not often deal in such illusions. Indeed, the burden of proof may be said to rest upon those who would deny that Rutebeuf really did have trouble with his right eye. Why otherwise would he have specified the *right* eye?[8] Similar

---

[7] 'De l'ueil destre, dont miex veoie, | Ne voi ge pas aleir la voie | Ne moi conduire', *La Complainte de Rutebeuf sur son Oeil*, lines 23–5, ed. Michel Zink, *Rutebeuf: Œuvres Complètes*, vol. i (Paris, 1989).

[8] Rutebeuf's most recent editor, Zink, discusses his 'mise en scène du moi' (ed. cit. 30). Zink expresses doubts about the autobiographical truth of Rutebeuf's various statements; yet his edition adopts a chronological order of the poems which assumes just that. See also his earlier book, Michel Zink, *La Subjectivité littéraire: Autour du siècle de Saint Louis* (Paris, 1985). Here he traces the emergence of the authorial *sujet* in 13th-cent. French writings, with valuable comments on the subjectivity of the *dit* and also (pp. 143 ff.) of dream allegory; but here too he may be suspected of an ideological

considerations may apply to Langland, and especially to the chief autobiographical, or 'autobiographical', passage in his poem, the scene between Will, Reason, and Conscience in C V. Admittedly, the name given to Will's wife at the beginning of this scene, 'Kit', is used elsewhere in the poem as a generic wife-name;[9] and the placing of their residence in Cornhill may have been meant to suggest nothing more than a certain unrespectability; but the ensuing account of Will's peculiar way of life cannot, I believe, be so easily accounted for. Indeed, so far is this way of life from falling into any recognizable general category that E. T. Donaldson has devoted the greater part of a chapter of his book to analysing it in all its singularity. Long Will emerges, in Donaldson's painstaking analysis, as 'a married clerk, of an order certainly no higher than acolyte, who made his living in an irregular fashion by saying prayers for the dead or for the living who supported him'.[10] It is precisely the irregularity of this life, as traced in detail by Donaldson, that lends force to his protest against 'regarding the passage as an obscurely motivated description of no one in particular' (p. 202); for why would an author—a medieval author, that is—have invented anything so singular? I think we may agree with Donaldson that, pending a satisfactory answer to that question, 'it seems best to assume that Langland was telling the truth about himself and not whimsically devising an elaborate fiction' (p. 220). Such an argument falls well short of the strict proof required by Kane; but it lends at least a decent minimum of support to those readers of the poem whose suspended judgement inclines towards belief.

Yet if one attempts to explore further into Langland's self-representations, his Self-Portrait as Long Will, other problems

---

bias against taking self-references as representing anything other than 'l'exhibition fictive du moi en poésie' (p. 171).

[9] C VII. 304. Kit is referred to as Will's wife also in B XVIII. 429 (C XX. 472), coupled there with a daughter named Calote. For a recent argument that the names, at least, are probably fictional, see Malcolm Godden, *The Making of Piers Plowman* (London, 1990), 9–10. The evidence that 'Kit callet' was a term of abuse in 16th-cent. English is particularly striking. See also T. F. Mustanoja, in J. Mandel and B. A. Rosenberg (eds.), *Medieval Literary and Folklore Studies in Honor of F. L. Utley* (New Brunswick, NJ, 1970), 73–4.

[10] *Piers Plowman: The C-Text and its Poet* (New Haven, Conn., 1949), 219.

arise; for one may then enter a territory where external
particulars, such as the poet's marital or occupational status,
are no longer in question, and where documentary evidence
is not even conceivably to be looked for. The Ricardian period
has, of course, left no literary memoirs of the sort that in a
later period allow us to form a conception of what Words-
worth or Coleridge was like in everyday life. We know that
Langland does, at least nominally, represent himself in his
poem; but how like Long Will are we to suppose him to have
been? The question is unavoidable, not because the man is
more interesting than his poem, but because one's response
to it, conscious or otherwise, must somewhat determine—as
it will also be determined by—any reading of the poem itself.
It is one thing, putting the alternatives at their starkest, to
read Long Will as a purely fictive persona whose charac-
teristics and responses are invented in order to further the
poem's purposes, and quite another to look in him for Lang-
land's very self.

A comparison may help to bring the problem into focus.
About the year 1350, Francis Petrarch wrote a Latin work,
the *Secretum*, in which he imagined three dialogues between
'Franciscus' and 'Augustinus'.[11] Petrarch's use of his baptismal
name, rather than his more distinctive surname, has a slight
generalizing effect; but his 'Franciscus' is, much more clearly
and continuously than Langland's Will, the author himself,
the historical Francis Petrarch imaginatively submitting him-
self to the scrutiny of that master of moral and spiritual
self-examination, the Augustine of the *Confessions*.[12] Thus, in
the second of the dialogues Augustinus, like a confessor but

---

[11] Ed. Enrico Carrara in G. Martellotti, P. G. Ricci, E. Carrara, and E. Bianchi
(eds.), *Francesco Petrarca, Prose* (Milan and Naples, 1955). Discussion by Kenelm Foster,
*Petrarch: Poet and Humanist* (Edinburgh, 1984), 161–85.

[12] One would like to know whether Langland had, like Petrarch, read the *Confessions*.
The Latin quotation assigned to 'Austyn ... in a sermon' at B X. 452a (A XI. 305, C
XI. 290a) in fact derives, albeit loosely, from *Confessions* VIII. 8. See C. David Benson,
'An Augustinian Irony in *Piers Plowman*', *Notes and Queries*, 221 (1976), 51–4; and
John A. Alford, *Piers Plowman: A Guide to the Quotations* (Binghamton, NY, 1992),
70. Among those who stress the relevance of the *Confessions* to Langland's poem are
Joseph S. Wittig, '*Piers Plowman* B, Passus IX–XII: Elements in the Design of the
Inward Journey', *Traditio*, 28 (1972), 211–80; 232–3, 245–8, 262–3; and Margaret E.
Goldsmith, *The Figure of Piers Plowman: The Image on the Coin* (Cambridge, 1981), 8–9
etc.

in a highly personal and informal manner, takes Franciscus
through an examination of the seven deadly sins; and under
each head it is clearly Petrarch's own particular life that is in
question. So, under Gluttony, Augustinus finds nothing to
notice except 'an occasional nice dinner party for the benefit
of friends', whereas he speaks at length, under Pride, of the
excessive confidence of Franciscus in his own intellect and his
'reading of many books'.[13] The comparable passage in *Piers
Plowman*, the confession of the Seven Deadly Sins in B V,
involves Will only in a much more marginal and uncertain
fashion, yet involve him it does. At the end of Reason's
sermon to the people, the confessor Repentance 'rehercedd his
teme | And garte Wille to wepe water with hise eighen' (V.
60–1). This may be taken as representing nothing more dis-
tinctive than the right response of any human will to a call
for repentance; but in the B Text—and in B only—there
occurs another and more singular reference to Will. After the
confession of Wrath, Repentance tells that sin to repent, to
keep private matters to himself, and to moderate his drink-
ing—

> 'That thi wille by cause therof to wrathe myghte turne.
> *Esto sobrius!*' he seide, and assoiled me after,
> And bad me wilne to wepe my wikkednesse to amende.[14]

Why should '*my* wikkednesse' figure here and here only, in
connection with the particular sin of wrath? It might be
regarded purely as contributing to the characterization of the
fictional Long Will; but among the faults displayed by the
dreamer in the poem anger is not so very conspicuous.
Alternatively, one may see here a moment of authorial self-
representation, betraying Langland's perception of one of his
own chief faults. But even those who incline to the latter

---

[13] Ed. Carrara, 96, 72. In his discussion of late medieval confessional practice as
a 'matrix of early Renaissance autobiography', T. C. Price Zimmerman observes that
the *Secretum* presents exchanges between confessor and penitent in the manner of a
classical dialogue: 'Confession and Autobiography in the Early Renaissance', in
Anthony Molho and John A. Tedeschi (eds.), *Renaissance: Studies in Honor of Hans Baron*
(Dekalb, Ill., and Florence, 1971), 119–40; 129–30.

[14] B V. 183–5. The whole Wrath episode is lacking in A. In C, the pronouns refer
to Wrath, not Will: ' "*Esto sobrius*," he seide, and assoiled hym aftur, | And bad hym
bid to God, be his help to amende' (C VI. 168–9).

reading, as I do, must recognize that it *is* only a moment, and as such hardly to be compared with the continuous, humanistic self-awareness displayed by Petrarch in the *Secretum*. *Piers Plowman* does not concern itself with particulars of its author's life and character in the same way as does the *Secretum*. Our sense of Langland's 'self' is derived more indirectly and uncertainly.

But how, we must ask at this point in the argument, should we understand that word 'self'? This is in fact a difficult matter, which has been much discussed in recent theoretical writings on the subject of autobiography. The general drift of these writings has been to question the common-sense assumption that there is such a thing as a fixed and identifiable self, by reference to which the veracity of a given literary self-portrait may be measured. Such theorists stress the processes by which an individual's selfhood will be formed and transformed in the course of encounters with others. There is that primary and continuing encounter with the society into which one is born and the language which it speaks; and there are also all those other encounters and relationships which cast the individual from time to time in a variety of more or less temporary roles.[15] Hence we may have our 'friend selves', our 'student selves', our 'mother selves', and the like. From this it seems to follow that a person who writes, and in the process of writing creates a 'writer self', is doing something no different in principle from what people do all the time. The 'persona', in other words, is in no way an exclusively literary phenomenon.[16]

[15] Thus, Paul John Eakin describes the autobiographical act as 'both a re-enactment and an extension of earlier phases of identity formation', *Fictions in Autobiography: Studies in the Art of Self-Invention* (Princeton, NJ, 1985), 226. See also James Olney (ed.), *Autobiography: Essays Theoretical and Critical* (Princeton, NJ, 1980). For a Marxist and materialist view, see Robert Elbaz, *The Changing Nature of the Self: A Critical Study of the Autobiographical Discourse* (London, 1988). Speaking of the self, Elbaz observes that 'the heart of the onion is but a series of peels' (p. 69). Relevant observations by psychologists may be found in David C. Rubin (ed.), *Autobiographical Memory* (Cambridge, 1986), especially in the essay by Craig R. Barclay on what he calls 'self-schemata' (pp. 82–99). For a social psychologist's view, see Erving Goffman's classic study, *The Presentation of Self in Everyday Life* (Harmondsworth, 1969). A somewhat sketchy philosopher's history of the self is given by Charles Taylor, *Sources of the Self: The Making of the Modern Identity* (Cambridge, 1989).

[16] A similar point is made by Stephen Greenblatt in his book *Renaissance Self-Fashioning* (Chicago, 1980), 3: 'self-fashioning derives its interest precisely from the fact that it functions without regard for the sharp distinction between literature and social life'.

If this is so, then it follows that, in considering what I have
called Langland's Self-Portrait as Long Will, we are faced with
something more complex than a straight alternative between
truth and fiction, *verité* and *mençonge*. It is not a simple either-or
problem, like the problem of whether the poet did or did not
live in Cornhill. There is no occasion to ask the impossible
question whether Langland did or did not in life play the
same roles and exhibit the same behaviour that he attributes
to Long Will in his poem. The right starting-point, rather, is
to recognize that, when Langland imagines himself as Long
Will, he is doing something which everyone does all the time
anyway. And surely the fact that this imagining of self occurs
in the process of writing a poem need not mean that it must
be considered as having some special secondary status. Why,
after all, should we insist that its sole claim to autobiographical
truth must derive from correspondence with the poet's every-
day presentations of self? On the contrary. In the case of a
poem so long and deeply pondered as *Piers Plowman*, at least,
we should surely allow the possibility that the 'fictions of self'
created in it may represent the poet's consciousness of his self
or selves at its most profound and searching. It may be, after
all, that Langland could have said of his poem what Michael
Montaigne said of his essays: 'I have no more made my booke,
then my booke hath made me. A booke consubstantiall to his
Author.'[17]

In speaking of Langland's self 'or selves' I had in mind the
variety of roles adopted and behaviours exhibited by his
persona Long Will in the course of the poem. Here I agree
with David Lawton, who has argued that it is just not possible
to understand Will as a single consistent 'character'. As Law-
ton says, Will displays 'a bewildering number of attributes',
and 'there are simply too many of these, some contradictory
and not all in play simultaneously, for the notion of charac-
terization to cope with'.[18] I agree with Lawton, too, that there

---

[17] *The Essayes of Michael Lord of Montaigne Translated by John Florio*, 6 vols. (London,
1897), Bk II, ch. 18, 'Of giving the lie'. Cf. Montaigne's preceding observation: 'In
framing this pourtraite by my selfe, I have so often beene faine to frizle [curl] and
trimme me, that so I might the better extract my selfe, that the patterne is thereby
confirmed, and in some sort formed' (ed. cit. IV. 187).
[18] 'The Subject of *Piers Plowman*', *Yearbook of Langland Studies*, 1 (1987), 1–30; 11.

is little to be gained from attempts to read the story of Will sequentially, as the history of a person's progress towards spiritual maturity. Long Will is indeed, as Lawton maintains, a 'discontinuous', 'plural' figure. At times he speaks as prophetic critic of the contemporary world, at times as anxious seeker after truth, and at other times as defender and justifier of himself. I regard all these as, in the sense I have tried to suggest, Langlandian fictions of self; but in what follows I shall confine myself to Will in just one of his roles. For the claim that *Piers Plowman* is 'a booke consubstantiall to his Author' can only be judged, one way or the other, on the evidence of the readings that, page by page, it promotes.

The remainder of this chapter is devoted to three episodes where the poet, in the person of Will, confronts his own poem, or rather is confronted by it. *Piers Plowman* contains much fierce criticism of contemporary Church and society; but in these episodes we see, I think, how the sheer critical intensity and moral idealism of the poem from time to time precipitate an equally unsparing criticism of self. By what right does Will set himself up as prophet and judge over his contemporaries? What business is it of his, indeed, to be writing the poem at all? Each of the episodes in question takes the form of an encounter between Will and personified abstractions: Imaginatif, Need, and Reason and Conscience. The encounters are imaginary, and some may choose to take them as pure inventions, designed to strengthen the moral impact of the poem. Certainly they do have the effect of making it difficult for readers to take shelter from the poem's severities by identifying with a blameless author. Yet the evidence of the poem itself—and what better evidence could there be?— speaks in favour, as I shall try to demonstrate, of a more personal interpretation. In defending his own moral position Will offers, and is offered, a variety of excuses; and it is as if the poet, in imagining these episodes of accusation and excusation, found himself able to articulate his most essential self, the self that creates the poem, and also to comprehend some of the difficult moral issues involved in that creation.

The first, unfinished version of the poem does not submit Will to the kind of interrogation I have in mind. The idea of doing so seems to have occurred to Langland in the process

of thinking about how he might proceed beyond the point
where the A Text broke off.[19] In the event, his very first step
in the B continuation is to confront Will, in his dream-within-
a-dream, with a monitory vision of his own life to date. In a
sequence based on a well-known passage in the First Epistle
of St John, Will sees himself pass from a fleshly youth through
a worldly middle age and so come face to face with the
deprivations of old age. Such a highly schematic and conven-
tionalized life history, at such a double remove from waking,
could hardly have anything but an exemplary significance; yet
when Will wakes from that inner dream it is as if he wakes
to find it true—even though he is, of course, still dreaming.
Now Imaginatif addresses him as a man who has indeed
passed through youth and middle age, and who presently
stands, at the age of 45, on the brink of the last of his three
ages, 'elde'.[20] So Imaginatif calls upon him to 'amende' and
reform his way of life. Will has received many warnings, but
has ignored them all; and even now, so late in his life, he is
spending precious time on the writing of poetry:

'. . . thow medlest thee with makynges—and myghtest go seye
    thi Sauter,
And bidde for hem that yyveth thee breed; for ther are bokes ynowe
To telle men what Dowel is, Dobet and Dobest bothe,
And prechours to preve what it is, of many a peire freres.'

                                                    (XII. 16–19)

One does not have to believe (as I do) that Langland was in
reality 45 years of age when he wrote these lines to see in
them something of his own reflections upon the poem that he
had recently resumed, and in particular upon that middle
section, as yet uncompleted, concerning Will's quest for
knowledge of Dowel. The whole scene between Will and
Imaginatif, with its accusations and countering excuses, seems

---

[19] I accept the biographical explanation given by R. W. Chambers for the
fragmentary form of the A Text—that Langland was at a loss how to continue it:
*Man's Unconquerable Mind* (London, 1939), 130–1.
[20] On the significance of 45 within schemes of the three ages of man, see J. A.
Burrow, 'Langland *Nel Mezzo del Cammin*', in P. L. Heyworth (ed.), *Medieval Studies for
J. A. W. Bennett* (Oxford, 1981), 21–41; also Middleton, 'William Langland's "Kynde
Name" ', 52–4.

designed to embody in dramatic form a somewhat turbulent mixture of conflicting thoughts and feelings.

Imaginatif is a figure of considerable authority, representing the mind's capacity to see beyond the present moment and take longer views.[21] In the lines just quoted he invokes, not just the general responsibility of an ageing man to care for his soul, but also a more particular responsibility resting upon Will—to 'bidde for hem that yyveth thee breed'. Langland does not enter here into the problematic question of his everyday occupation: that is treated in the episode in the C Text to be discussed later. The present passage implies no more than that Will's way of life is such that he owes a return of prayers to those who give him food—like Chaucer's Clerk of Oxenford, who 'bisily gan for the soules preye | Of hem that yaf hym wherwith to scoleye'. But the accusations are gathering force. A man on the threshold of old age, and especially a man dependent upon others for his bread, has no business to be 'meddling with makings' and so neglecting his obligations both to his benefactors and to his own soul. What is more, Will's poetical labours are not just irresponsible for a man of his age and circumstances; they are also superfluous. There are already quite enough books on his chosen subject, and enough sermons too.

Yet the last phrase of Imaginatif's speech raises an unsettling doubt: 'And prechours to preve what it is, of many a peire freres'. Langland does not elsewhere treat the truth about Dowel as something to be easily learned from books; and certainly the claim that the friars, of all people, can be relied upon to 'preve what it is' runs counter to much else in the poem. Mendicant preachers are elsewhere commonly associated with specious theological questions, 'glosing', and the like. Even when they preach wholesome doctrine, contrasts between their pious words and unscrupulous conduct are a source of scandal to the right-thinking observer. Such is the gluttonous friar doctor who pontificates about Dowel at Conscience's dinner party. Is that the kind of thing that renders Langland's poem redundant? 'Preve' is a pregnant word in

---

[21] Wittig, '*Piers Plowman* B, Passus IX–XII', 272–3, convincingly takes Imaginatif to represent the activity of 'representing vividly to oneself'.

*Piers Plowman.* A friar may be able to 'preve' what Dowel is
in words; but, unlike Piers himself, he will not undertake to
'preve this in dede', demonstrate it in action (XIII. 132). Not
that Langland does either; but the words of his poem do
represent a strenuous effort to pay more than lip-service to
the ideal.

In his reply, Will acknowledges the force of Imaginatif's
accusations, but counters them with excuses:

> I seigh wel he seide me sooth and, somwhat me to excuse,
> Seide, 'Caton conforted his sone that, clerk though he were,
> To solacen hym som tyme—also I do whan I make:
> *Interpone tuis interdum gaudia curis.*
> And of holy men I herde,' quod I, 'how thei outherwhile
> Pleyden, the parfiter to ben, in places manye.
> Ac if ther were any wight that wolde me telle
> What were Dowel and Dobet and Dobest at the laste,
> Wolde I nevere do werk, but wende to holi chirche
> And there bidde my bedes but whan ich ete or slepe.'
> 
> (XII. 20–8)

What should one make of these excuses? It seems strange that
Will should choose to justify his long and difficult poem as a
mere *gaudium*, a solace or pastime, of the sort recommended
by Dionysius Cato to his student son: 'Give place sometimes
for pleasures among your cares [so that you may have the
spirit to sustain your labours].' The Distichs of Cato, a school
textbook of the time, was no mean authority to cite; and this
particular distich (recalled by Milton in *Lycidas*, 'interpose a
little ease') expresses a belief in the restorative power of
recreation, poetry included, that was widely held then, as
now.[22] So Will's argument for the recreational utility of his
'making' carries more weight than might at first appear. Yet
it is hard not to believe that he is getting somewhat carried
away when he goes on to cite the precedent of holy men and
so associate himself with their aspiration to perfection, no less.
As we shall see, he is rapped over the knuckles by Conscience
in the C passage for speaking of himself as a 'perfect' man.

---

[22] See Glending Olson, *Literature as Recreation in the Later Middle Ages* (Ithaca, NY,
1982), esp. 93–4 on *Disticha*, III. 6.

Langland comes close here, as Ricardian poets often do, to mocking himself.

Yet Will's final remark surely demands to be taken seriously:

> 'Ac if ther were any wight that wolde me telle
> What were Dowel and Dobet and Dobest at the laste,
> Wolde I nevere do werk, but wende to holi chirche
> And there bidde my bedes but whan ich ete or slepe.'

The conditional clause here asserts the seriousness of Will's quest for Dowel (his writing is not merely recreational), and also rebuts Imaginatif's suggestion that there is no need for such a quest: 'You say that there are plenty of books and friars to tell me what Dowel is; but if only someone really would tell me . . .'. Will must be in earnest here. He does indeed want to know, not just what clever men can tell him, but something deeper and truer—the 'kind knowing' of which he elsewhere speaks. Yet as the sentence progresses, new doubts arise. If only someone would tell him . . . he would abandon the poem at once and take up a way of life in which neither work nor recreation would have any place—a life of continuous prayer, interrupted only by meals and sleep. Imaginatif could not possibly ask for more. Or perhaps he could? He has accused Will of persistently putting off the moment when he reforms his way of life: Will has gone on procrastinating until now, when it is almost too late. So perhaps the present is just another typical act of procrastination—a high-minded and grandiose resolution which Will may never have to act on so long as he refuses to recognize that his requirement has in fact been met long since. Such seems to be the hidden force of Imaginatif's uncompromising response to his flurry of excuses:

> 'Poul in his pistle,' quod he, 'preveth what is Dowel:
> *Fides, spes, caritas, et maior horum &c.*'

Will may be forgiven for refusing to be content with the testimony of friars; but what if he claims, as he surely will, that even St Paul's classic formulation fails to satisfy him?

The second of these subtle and elusive episodes of accusation and excuse occurs towards the end of the poem, in both B and C Texts. Here, in a waking interlude between his last

two dreams, Will is confronted by a personification called
'Need': B XX. 1–51. The passage has been much discussed,
especially in its relation to apocalyptic and anti-fraternal
themes in the dream which ensues—Need being considered
as a spokesman, for better or worse, for the friars' doctrine
of poverty and mendicancy.[23] However, Need's opening words
point back rather to the previous dream; and it is in this other
connection that the episode can, I think, best be understood:

> Thanne as I wente by the way, whan I was thus awaked,
> Hevy chered I yede, and elenge in herte;
> For I ne wiste wher to ete ne at what place,
> And it neghed neigh the noon, and with Nede I mette,
> That afrounted me foule and faitour me called.
> 'Coudestow noght excuse thee, as dide the kyng and othere—
> That thow toke to thy bilyve, to clothes and to sustenaunce,
> Was by techynge and by tellynge of *Spiritus Temperancie*,
> And that thow nome na moore than nede thee taughte . . . ?'
>
> (XX. 1–9)

'Coudestow noght excuse thee, as dide the kyng and othere?'
Need is offering Will an excuse—an excuse which, according
to Need, he could and should have employed on his own
behalf in the immediately preceding dream scene where the
king and others had offered their excuses. In that scene,
Conscience had invited the faithful to enter Holy Church and
partake with him of the eucharistic repast (XIX. 386–93); but
he will admit to his table only those who 'lyve by loore of
*Spiritus Iusticie*' and of the other cardinal virtues (408–11). This
condition means, in particular, that they should have 'paid
what they owe' in accordance with the terms of Piers's pardon
(XIX. 392–3). All kinds of 'debts' must have been duly settled:
they must have made restitution (394–6), have forgiven others
debts owed to them (397), and have fulfilled their obligation
to 'labour lelly' for their own livelihood (387).[24] This call for

---

[23] See Robert Adams, 'The Nature of Need in *Piers Plowman* XX', *Traditio*, 34
(1978), 273–301, and esp. Penn R. Szittya, *The Antifraternal Tradition in Medieval Literature*
(Princeton, NJ, 1986), 268–76. Also Kathryn Kerby-Fulton, *Reformist Apocalypticism and
Piers Plowman* (Cambridge, 1990), 146–9.

[24] Myra Stokes stresses here, as throughout her study, Langland's concern with the
'principle of equity', *Justice and Mercy in Piers Plowman: A Reading of the B Text Visio*
(London, 1984), 275–7.

a total settlement of spiritual and material accounts according to the 'loore of *Spiritus Iusticie*' causes general consternation among the people. A brewer will have nothing to do with Conscience and his feast on such terms; but two others, a lord and a king, offer those 'excuses' to which Need later refers. These are not excuses in the ordinary modern sense of the word: the lord and the king are not excusing themselves from participation in the feast.[25] On the contrary, they wish to be admitted to it; and their arguments are designed to show that they cannot justly be excluded on the ground of obligations unfulfilled. Each maintains that he has a right in justice to take what he takes from his estate or his kingdom to live by (462-7, 469-79), and so cannot fairly be held to owe an unsettled debt for what was rightfully his in the first place.

There is a close and subtle connection between these excuses and those offered by Need to the waking Will. It may appear from the opening lines of Passus XX, quoted above, that Will is more concerned about getting his lunch than about eating God's body; but Need in fact refers back to the latter; and in any case, the two kinds of meal are both subject, in Langland's mind, to the same conditions. The spirit of justice dictates that neither can be had, as it were, for free. In the face of this condition Will's case, like that of the lord and the king, and for exactly the same reason, appears dubious enough to require 'excuse'; for all three of them are takers rather than earners of their livelihoods. The words 'taken' and 'nimen' are key terms in all three passages of excuse: XIX. 463, 466 (the lord), XIX. 471, 476, 476 (the king), XX. 7, 9, 11, 20 (Need, on Will's behalf). Whereas the lord and the king are 'takers' by virtue of their high standing in society, Will—as Need represents him here—is reduced to taking by sheer destitution. He is evidently one of those whom Need describes, with the precision of an expert, as having no money, no backers, and nothing to pawn (XX. 12-13). So he has no alternative but to 'take', according to Need, and is justified in doing so. He could indeed have 'excused himself'.

---

[25] In this respect the episode reverses Luke's parable of the supper, from attendance at which the invitees excuse themselves: Luke 14: 16-24. An episode added in the C Text is based on this parable more directly: C VII. 292-304.

But how good are the excuses that Need offers Will? Would they have passed muster with Conscience? The answer is by no means obvious. Commonly, when personifications speak, their names (Patience, Wrath) guide the response to what they say, one way or another; but Need here represents, or so I believe, nothing other than the state of necessitous deprivation in which Will evidently finds himself, not knowing where the next meal is coming from. Need in itself is neither good nor bad, morally speaking.[26] So one is left to judge the arguments on their own merits. The main argument, so far as concerns Will, is that stated by Need in lines 7–22: that it is legitimate for one suffering extreme deprivation to take whatever he needs in the way of food, drink, and clothing, provided only that he observes the rule of temperance. He must, that is, take no more than the bare essentials needful to preserve life. This may seem no better than a dubious defence of theft; but it is, in fact, supported by passages elsewhere in the poem. Thus, although the first pardon sent to Piers excluded most beggars, it did not exclude those who take from others out of genuine need:

> For he that beggeth or bit, but if he have nede,
> He is fals with the feend and defraudeth the nedy.
>
> (VII. 66–7)

Again, Holy Church herself granted an absolute right to food, drink, and clothing 'at nede', and anticipated Need's proviso about temperance when she spoke of the 'mesurable manere' in which that right is to be enjoyed (I. 17–19). Even the most apparently provocative of Need's statements, that 'nede ne hath no lawe', does no more than repeat a commonly accepted maxim: *necessitas non habet legem*.[27]

Yet the matter can hardly be left there. Turning back again to that dream scene from which the Need episode springs, we

---

[26] It will be evident that I do not agree with Robert Adams, who identifies Need with the *egestas* of Job 41: 13 and describes him as 'a frighteningly active evangelist, an inverted John the Baptist preparing the way for his false master, Antichrist' ('The Nature of Need', 295).

[27] Langland cites the Latin maxim at C XIII. 43a. For other English examples, see B. J. and H. W. Whiting, *Proverbs, Sentences, and Proverbial Phrases from English Writings Mainly before 1500* (Cambridge, Mass., 1968), N51. See Morton W. Bloomfield, *Piers Plowman as a Fourteenth-Century Apocalypse* (New Brunswick, NJ, n.d. [1961]), 136.

find a world in which 'excuses' are very far from being above suspicion. There is, admittedly, no reason to suppose that Langland doubted the right of lords and kings to live from the proceeds of an estate or kingdom, and Conscience does himself allow at least the king's excuse, albeit conditionally— on condition that he rules justly and defends the realm from its enemies (XIX. 480–3).[28] Yet the excuses of the lord and the king immediately follow a speech by a 'lewed vicory' which seems calculated to cast a shadow across them. The vicar concludes with these words:

> '. . . *Spiritus Prudencie* among the peple is gyle,
> And alle tho faire vertues, as vices thei semeth.
> Ech man subtileth a sleighte synne to hide,
> And coloureth it for a konnynge and a clene lyvynge.'
>
> (XIX. 458–61)

So to invoke the cardinal virtues, as the lord, the king, and Need all do, may be nothing better than a deceitful 'sleighte', designed to hide and 'coloure' a sinful intention. Need's arguments were, in fact, commonly held to be misused by friars in this very fashion, to justify a life of idle and self-indulgent mendicancy.[29] So if, as the context requires, we imagine these same arguments in the mouth of Will, addressing Conscience, they produce a distinctly equivocal effect. Our response must depend upon whether or not we can accept Will's right to use such excuses in his own particular circumstances. Certainly, if we doubt that right, the latter part of Need's speech, with its high-sounding praise of temperance and poverty, will appear distinctly suspect—a case, perhaps, of 'subtiling a sleighte synne to hide'. The same suspicion, as we shall shortly see, is aroused by the equally eloquent excuses that Will offers Conscience and Reason in Passus V of the C Text. Everything depends, as always in *Piers Plowman*, upon the condition of the will—in this case, Will—and that is no easy matter to judge. Indeed, the present episode offers no

---

[28] At line 482, both Kane–Donaldson (see their p. 175) and Schmidt (pp. 301–2) emend the B archetype on the strength of C. However, the archetype's reading, though it lacks alliteration, provides another example of the key term 'take', very aptly used: 'Take thow mayst in reson as thi lawe asketh.'

[29] See Szittya, *The Antifraternal Tradition*, 270–2.

judgement at all, for it ends abruptly and without comment. Will does not respond to Need's reproaches, and plunges straight into his last dream.

Will's encounter with Need is strangely lacking in consequence. In his ensuing dream Will does eventually enter Holy Church, but then only at the last minute, when bodily decay and the fear of death drive him to it (XX. 183–213). The Need episode, as it turns out, is to play no part in the story of his ultimate and quite unheroic role in the history of man's salvation. So why is it there at all? Perhaps it is best understood as a partial and unsatisfactory attempt at something Langland was to do much more decisively in the C Text. When he came to make that version, he cut out the B-Text encounter with Imaginatif; and it may be that he would also have cut the much less successful Need episode, if he had got round (as he evidently never did) to revising his last two passus. For in the C-Text scene, to which I now turn, Langland's doubts about his own way of life—obscurely adumbrated in the Need episode—achieve definitive expression in a last, masterly fiction of self.

Will's exchanges with Reason and Conscience in C V take place, like his scene with Need, in a waking interlude between dreams. Langland had already, in the Imaginatif episode, employed a shift from inner to outer dream to mark a stepping back into consideration of self; and the further shift from dream to waking could evidently be used in the same way. The distinction between Will asleep and Will awake is, of course, not the same as that between fictional narrator and real-life poet; but the one relationship is homologous with the other, and suggestively so. Hence Will's encounter with Need could suggest, however obscurely, something of the poet's sense of his own uncertain standing in relation to the matter of the adjacent dreams—nothing less, in that case, than the current history of salvation itself. In C V, the issue is similarly set by the dreams between which the episode is placed: the dream of Lady Meed which precedes it, and that of the pilgrimage to Truth which follows. Will's two accusers, Reason and Conscience, step straight out of the former, but their questionings relate more closely to the latter, and especially to issues raised in the scene on the half acre. Piers the

Plowman will there insist that everyone should earn the livelihood that society affords them, so far as they are able, by making a legitimate contribution of one sort or another. But what sort of contribution does Will himself make? Such is Reason's question, and it provokes one of Langland's most brilliant passages—poetry of tough and sinuous argument, witty and richly detailed, in which the inner drama of accusation and excuse takes at last its definitive form.

The scene opens with an intriguing Self-Portrait as Long Will:

> Thus y awakede, woet God, whan y wonede in Cornehull,
> Kytte and y in a cote, yclothed as a lollare,
> And lytel ylet by, leveth me for sothe,
> Amonges lollares of Londone and lewede ermytes,
> For y made of tho men as Resoun me tauhte.
> For as y cam by Consience with Resoun y mette
> In an hot hervest whenne y hadde myn hele
> And lymes to labory with and lovede wel fare
> And no dede to do but to drynke and to slepe.
>
> (C V. 1–9)

A 'lollare' is an idler or loller about, and in particular one who exploits religion as an excuse for not working. Will has attacked such people in his verses ('made of tho men'), and so now is unpopular with them—a reference, it seems, to the reception of some already-circulated part of *Piers Plowman* itself.[30] Yet it is not easy to see how his own way of life, as portrayed here, can be distinguished from theirs. 'Yclothed as a lollare' may suggest that he only looks as if he might be a loller; yet the appearances are certainly damning. Will is fit and healthy, but even in this harvest season, a time of exceptional labour for many, his mind is set on a soft life of

---

[30] See Wendy Scase, 'Two *Piers Plowman* C-Text Interpolations: Evidence for a Second Textual Tradition', *Notes and Queries*, 232 (1987), 456–63; and her book, '*Piers Plowman' and the New Anticlericalism* (Cambridge, 1989), 149–50. The reference, according to Scase, is to some verses on the 'classification of beggars', first circulated separately, and subsequently incorporated into the C Text as C IX. 66–281. If she is right, this is striking evidence of identification between dreamer and poet; yet in general Scase treats what she calls the figure of 'the Cornhill loller' as a 'mask' adopted by the poet for purposes of anticlerical satire: see her book, pp. 125–60 and 172. Although I do not agree with Scase here, her discussion of the episode provides much valuable information, e.g. on the word 'loller' (pp. 150–7).

drink and sleep. It is easy enough, as Imaginatif suggested, to
'meddle with makings'; but practising what one preaches is
evidently a different matter. So the same Reason that guided
Will in his attacks on his neighbours now turns to attack their
author.

To begin with, Reason offers Will some possible excuses,
just as Need had done. Will seems, he says, to be himself an
idle man, living a loller's life; but perhaps, he wonders, the
poet may none the less be performing some real service for
the good society about which he writes so well. Reason is
being reasonable, but his generous catalogue of considerations
'whereby thow myhte be excused' amounts, in the end, to a
silkily ironic indictment:

> 'Can thow serven,' he sayde, 'or syngen in a churche,
> Or koke for my cokeres or to þe cart piche,
> Mowen or mywen or make bond to sheves,
> Repe or been a rypereve and aryse erly,
> Or have an horn and be hayward and lygge þeroute nyhtes
> And kepe my corn in my croft fro pykares and theves,
> Or shap shon or cloth, or shep and kyne kepe,
> Heggen or harwen, or swyn or gees dryve . . . ?'
>
> (C V. 12–19)

The sequence of closely allied activities in hayfield and corn-
field—appropriate to the harvest season—suggests by exten-
sion the long list of worthy crafts open to Will: he could make
hay-cocks, or fork hay into the cart, or mow hay, or stack it
in the barn, or reap corn, or oversee the reaping of it, or
guard it as a hayward . . . The list seems, and is meant to
seem, endless. Reason's pairs of closely similar but distinct
words indicate plural possibilities even in what might seem a
single occupation: 'koking' is evidently not quite the same as
being a 'cokere', 'mowing' is different from 'mywing', and a
'rypereve' is not a 'reper'. The same effect, of numerous small
but distinguishable permutations of craft, is created by the
subtle play of sounds, characteristic of Langland's poetry at
its best, in the line 'Or shap shon or cloth, or shep and kyne
kepe', where 'shape' becomes 'sheep', which in turn becomes
'keep' by exchanging its initial consonant with 'kine'. All these
are Reason's own crafts (*my* cockers, *my* corn, *my* croft), and

he sets them before Will with evident relish. How can Will, faced with such a wealth of possibilities, fail to find something to suit him?

But none of Reason's proffered excuses can serve for Will; so he has to find his own. His first defensive position, prompted by Reason's catalogue of agricultural jobs, is to claim that he is too weak and too tall for work in the harvest field. His height is elsewhere vôuched for by his nickname, 'Long Will'; and his claim to be weak is not, strictly speaking, incompatible with his previously announced possession of health and 'limbs to labour with'. Yet these excuses, for what they are worth, will serve only for fieldwork and the like; so in a later, longer speech Will falls back on a more comprehensive defence. He claims privilege of clergy, describing his schooling as a clerk and his present way of life in accordance with that vocation. He prays for the souls of his benefactors, and his clerkly 'tools' are religious texts. Will goes on to admit that he might be called a beggar, but only in an acceptable sense: he follows the precepts of Need in accepting from his patrons only what he can carry away in his belly, and he repays them with his prayers, just as Imaginatif required.

One should, I think, be uncertain what to make of these excuses; and in what follows, uncertainty is compounded. Will launches into a tirade in defence of clerical privilege, and this widens out into a general attack on the breakdown of social order in modern times, ending on an apocalyptic note:

> 'Lyf-holynesse and love hath be longe hennes,
> And wol, til hit be wered out, or oþerwyse ychaunged.'

The reader of *Piers Plowman* will recognize much that is familiar in this tirade, for many of its sentiments are echoed elsewhere in the poem. Certainly Will's conservative view of contemporary society is Langland's own. Yet, if Will speaks for Langland here, that may in the present context suggest rather doubts about Langland than confidence in Will. There is even a suggestion of self-parody—a subtle placing of the poet's own favourite sentiments—and that suggestion grows more distinct as Will's speech rises to its triumphant conclusion:

'Forthy rebuke me ryhte nauhte, Resoun, y ʒow praye,
For in my consience y knowe what Crist wolde y wrouhte.
Preyeres of a parfit man and penaunce discret
Is the levest labour þat oure lord pleseth.
*Non de solo*,' y sayde, 'for sothe *vivit homo*,
*Nec in pane et in pabulo*, the *pater-noster* wittenesseth;
*Fiat voluntas Dei*—þat fynt us alle thynges.'

(C V. 82–8)

So Will now claims that his life of prayers and penance is
more than just an acceptable vocation: his is actually the work
most pleasing of all to God. And he caps that exalted claim,
very much in Langland's general manner, with two biblical
texts to prove that God will provide: 'Man does not live by
bread alone, but by every word that proceeds from the mouth
of God', and, from the Lord's Prayer, 'God's will be done'.
Patience elsewhere uses the same texts in support of the same
high spiritual doctrine, in addressing Hawkin the Active
Man;[31] but Will, unlike Patience, indulges himself in a little
clerkly wit. He recasts the first text (Matthew 4: 4) in such a
way that the word *solo*, instead of its Vulgate use as an
adjective agreeing with *pane* ('bread alone'), stands apart as a
noun—the noun *solum*, meaning 'soil'. So the quotation now
glances back, with a kind of exultant irony, at Reason's earlier
talk of fieldwork: 'Not from the soil does man live, nor by
bread and by food.'

By this stage the scene has developed considerable tension,
between the powerful Langlandian rhetoric and the dubious
purpose to which it seems here to be put. So the brisk
rejoinder from Conscience serves to clear the air:

Quod Consience, 'By Crist, y can nat se this lyeth;
Ac it semeth no sad parfitnesse in citees to begge,
But he be obediencer to prior or to mynistre.'

(89–91)

Will has claimed, by implication, that he is living the life of
'a parfit man'; but Conscience does not see that this claim
can be admitted ('lyeth') in his particular case.[32] Will's life, as

---

[31] C XV. 245a, 250; B XIV. 47a, 49.
[32] Malcolm Godden takes 'lyeth' to mean 'lies, is untrue' here: *RES* NS 35 (1984),
155; but the legalistic use of the word has more pointed sense here: *OED Lie* v[1], sense

he himself describes it, 'semeth no sad parfitnesse'. Here 'sad' is a pregnant word, meaning something like 'settled', 'regular', or 'serious'. 'Obediencers' may legitimately go about making collections for religious houses, but Will's begging rounds have no such authority. Being irregular, or governed by no rule, they are highly suspect. It is appropriate that it should be Conscience, speaking here for the first time in the scene, who is called upon to make this point; for, where reason understands general principles, conscience applies them to particular cases. 'Conscientia nihil aliud est quam applicatio scientiae ad aliquem actum.'[33]

Will is capable of recognizing the truth when it is displayed to him: he did so with Imaginatif, and he does so now. Acknowledging that Conscience is right, he confesses that he has misspent his life, and expresses the fervent hope that he may yet have grace to amend:

> 'That is soth,' y saide, 'and so y beknowe
> That y have ytynt tyme and tyme myspened;
> Ac ʒut I hope, as he þat ofte hath ychaffared
> And ay loste and loste, and at þe laste hym happed
> A bouhte suche a bargayn he was þe bet evere,
> And sette al his los at a leef at the laste ende,
> Suche a wynnyng hym warth thorw wordes of grace—
>    *Simile est regnum celorum thesauro abscondito in agro;*
>    *Mulier que invenit dragmam etc.*—
> So hope y to have of hym þat is almyghty
> A gobet of his grace, and bigynne a tyme
> That alle tymes of my tyme to profit shal turne.'[34]

It is a majestic and moving speech of repentance and resolution—a single sustained rhetorical period, ending as it began

---

13, '(Chiefly in *Law*) Of an action, charge, claim, etc.: To be admissible or sustainable'. See also *MED lien* v.(1),' sense 11(b). E. T. Donaldson sees a deliberate ambiguity between the two meanings: 'Conscience's *double entendre* characterizes Long Will's apology as at once specious and heart-felt, false and true': 'Long Will's Apology: A Translation', in Gregory Kratzmann and James Simpson (eds.), *Medieval English Religious and Ethical Literature: Essays in Honour of G. H. Russell* (Cambridge, 1986), 30–4; 32. Donaldson's brief discussion of the 'apology' here is noteworthy.

[33] Thomas Aquinas, *Summa Theologica*, I–II q.19 a.5: 'Conscience is nothing other than the application of knowledge to a certain act.'

[34] C v. 92–101. I have altered Pearsall's punctuation to show the whole passage quoted as one sentence, with the 'so hope y' of line 99 recapitulating the 'I hope' of line 94.

with clangorous repetition of the key word 'time': 'bigynne a tyme | That alle tymes of my tyme to profit shal turne'. All Will's wasted moments may, with God's grace, be redeemed in a single moment, all his many losses be wiped out by one great winning. The possibility is vouched for by the two parables of Christ evoked in the Latin texts, and also by the parable of the merchant which Will himself invents.

The scene might well have ended on that note; but Langland's moral imagination is at full power in this passage, and Will's exalted utterance provokes two laconic rejoinders:

> 'Y rede the,' quod Resoun tho, 'rape the to bigynne
> The lyif þat is louble and leele to thy soule'—
> 'ʒe, and contynue,' quod Consience; and to ʒe kyrke y wente.

Picking up Will's rhapsodic hope to begin a new time, Reason drily advises him to hurry up and begin, then. The implicit comment does not exactly invalidate Will's resolution; but it checks that speech of his with the thought that hopes and resolutions—as the encounter with Imaginatif also suggested— can too easily take the place of action. Conscience follows this up even more laconically. Will had earlier spoken of a life good for the soul 'by so y wol contenue', that is, 'provided I persevere in it' (line 39). It is to this that Conscience now refers: 'And when (if?) you do begin, make sure that you persevere.' On that warning note the episode concludes, and Will goes to church to pray and repent his sins.

In these readings of three passages from *Piers Plowman*, I have treated Langland's Self-Portraits as Long Will as if they represented acts of real self-questioning on the poet's part— albeit acts disciplined and to an indeterminate degree fictionalized by the exigencies of art, as self-portraits, and especially self-portraits *in maschera*, necessarily are. Professor George Kane, a scholar who knows the poem perhaps better than anyone alive, has recently attacked what he describes as a romantic fallacy, 'the attempt to recreate a historical Langland from the attributes of his dreamer'.[35] However, it has been my contention that no one can in reality read or discuss *Piers*

---

[35] 'Langland and Chaucer II', in George Kane, *Chaucer and Langland: Historical and Textual Approaches* (London, 1989), 147.

*Plowman* without doing just that—'recreating a historical Lang-
land', shaped in accordance with their reading of the text.
Professor Kane himself is no exception to this. Indeed, on the
very same page of the essay from which I have quoted, he
clearly projects his own image—albeit a very *un*romantic
image—of what the historical Langland was like. 'On grounds
of both literary convention and the substance of his poem,
which is unmistakably for an educated audience, the likelihood
is that Langland exploited the illusion of the authorial per-
sonality as much as Chaucer did. He was clearly writing for
readers united in the concerns registered in his poem, prob-
ably educated clergy anxious for ecclesiastical reform, and I
would guess that he wrote from within that group. There is
little chance that his audience, recognizing how the author
writes all the parts and manipulates all the puppets, would
unthinkingly impute to him the Dreamer Will's recurrent
spiral of anxieties about grace and works, predestination,
original sin and divine justice to the poet in any simple way,
or read the poem as a record of the poet's own search for
salvation, as a *Bildungsroman*.'[36] I agree that one should not
impute Will's anxieties to the poet himself 'unthinkingly' or
in a 'simple way'; but when Kane speaks of Langland writing
all the parts and manipulating all the puppets, he is surely
himself offering us a version of the historical Langland. The
theatrical and puppeteering metaphors suggest a poet de-
tached and perfectly in command of his own thoughts and
beliefs—as befits, perhaps, a member of the 'educated clergy'
writing for an 'educated audience'. It is not to the purpose
here to dispute this image of Langland. The point is simply
that Kane's own version of what the poet was like depends
just as much as its perhaps more 'romantic' rivals upon
inferences from the text ('I would guess . . .'). So those who
find it difficult to read Will's encounters with Reason, Con-
science, and the rest as intellectual puppet-theatre are under
no particular obligation to do so. It remains, one way or
another, a matter of critical opinion.

To conclude this discussion somewhat in Langland's own
manner, let me quote another authority *contra* Professor Kane.

[36] Ibid.

Of the C-Text episode between Will, Reason, and Conscience, Rosemary Woolf (herself a good literary historian, and no romantic) wrote as follows: 'The passage does not have the general relevance nor the unmistakable borrowing of previous commonplaces which occurred in the passage describing the ageing of the dreamer, so that if it does not contain genuine personal description, it is difficult to account for it. But if it is personal description, then we can see clearly in it Langland's self-conscious concern and uncertainty over himself, of which the whole poem could in a sense be called a magnificent extension. It may well be that it was Langland's passionate concern with his own difficulties and their relationship to wider issues which was the driving force of the poem, contributing to both its merits and defects.'[37]

---

[37] Rosemary Woolf, 'Some Non-Medieval Qualities of *Piers Plowman*', *Essays in Criticism*, 12 (1962), 111–25. I quote from pp. 94–5 of the reprint in Woolf, *Art and Doctrine: Essays on Medieval Literature*, ed. Heather O'Donoghue (London, 1986). Woolf regarded such self-portraiture as untypical of medieval writers; but this is questioned by Kerby-Fulton, *Reformist Apocalypticism*, 116. Kerby-Fulton argues that the background to Langland's self-portraits is to be looked for in the Latin religious visionary tradition. See also her pp. 64–75 on the 'visionary self-image'.

# CHAPTER 5

# Afterword

In the foregoing discussions of Langland's dream fictions I have not been concerned to maintain their resemblance to actual dream experience (whatever that experience may have been like in the fourteenth century). Yet the dream settings of *Piers Plowman* do play an essential role there, for they serve to define the epistemological status of the poem's contents— more subtly so, I think, than in any other medieval English dream poem. They act as an index or standing guarantee of fictive status, as if the relation between dream and waking corresponded to, and so could represent, the relation between fiction and truth: fiction stands to truth as dream to waking. Though *Piers* demands to be read as the work of an author profoundly concerned with thinking about truth—especially about the conditions of salvation for himself and his contemporaries—yet it is also of the poem's essence, I have argued, that such concerns should manifest themselves in the form of fictions, just as waking experience manifests itself in the worlds of dream. In both, it is the imagination that 'says as it sees'.

But if Langland's thinking about himself, his society, and his God expresses itself in the poem through dream fictions, what essential difference does that make? How does the thinking itself differ from what one would have expected in a non-fictional treatise? One rather negative answer suggests itself. An analytic treatise on what the poem calls 'Dowel' might have canvassed a variety of possible accounts or definitions, but it could hardly have failed to arrive at some proffered conclusion. Yet Long Will's search for just such a conclusion, extending from Passus VIII to XIII, never arrives at one. What *is* that way of life upon which our hope of salvation largely depends? The poem does, of course, offer answers; but Will's inability to be satisfied with any one of them represents—partially hidden under a mask of dreamerly 'dullness'—a real refusal, or failure, on the author's part to commit himself to any definitive formulation. The matter is,

in the event, not so much resolved as shelved, and the poem
proceeds to focus on other terms (patience, charity). But that,
it has been said, is precisely one of the special privileges of
fiction: to treat a problem as 'undecidable'.[1]

Yet to evade decision is hardly the main function of Lang-
land's dream fictions. In some of them, including some of
those discussed in Chapter 2, the story serves to convey a
judgement more delicately balanced than could well be con-
veyed, with any number of qualifying *acs*, in discursive prose.
In the dinner scene in Passus XIII, the parting exchanges
between Clergy and Conscience define Langland's mixed
feelings about the clerical establishment with a precision that
makes Imaginatif's earlier discussion of the matter look rather
ham-fisted. Similarly, the scene with Reason and Conscience
in C V stands as a convincing monument, or so I believe, to
the poet's mixed feelings about himself. These are examples
of what Wesley Trimpi calls the 'equitable function' of fic-
tion—its capacity, that is, to show general ethical principles
in their flexible application to the circumstances of a particular
case. In his remarkable book, *Muses of One Mind*, Trimpi shows
how this function of fiction was understood in the rhetorical
and legal traditions inherited by the Middle Ages from classi-
cal antiquity.[2]

Yet, if one thinks in particular of the figure of Piers
Plowman himself, one must recognize that not all Langland's
fictions are susceptible of fully rational analysis. Rosemary
Woolf wrote of Piers that he has 'the peculiar force of
something which is only half understood'; and nothing in
Langland criticism, before or since, has succeeded in dispelling
that opacity.[3] Certainly it is possible to mark the perimeter,

[1] Frank Lentricchia, *After the New Criticism* (London, 1980), 349: 'As self-conscious fictionality or undecidability, poetic power represents, with respect to the basic domination, an underside that is doomed to perpetual defeat, to perpetually empty gestures of literary freedom.'

[2] Wesley Trimpi, *Muses of One Mind: The Literary Analysis of Experience and its Continuity* (Princeton, NJ, 1983), Part Three, 'The Quality of Fiction: The Rhetorical Trans-mission of Literary Theory', esp. 252–8 ('Fiction and the *Status Qualitatis*').

[3] 'Some Non-Medieval Qualities of *Piers Plowman*', in Woolf, *Art and Doctrine*, 87. The most recent attempt to define what Piers represents is by Samuel A. Overstreet, 'Langland's Elusive Plowman', *Traditio*, 45 (1989–90), 257–341. 'Patient poverty of heart' is Overstreet's answer.

as it were, of the Plowman's significance by noting what
Langland opposes him to—book-learning, for instance—but
there remains within that perimeter an apparently irreducible
core of mystery. Here, and in several other places in *Piers
Plowman*, the term 'fiction' seems altogether too cold-blooded;
and one can understand why Geoffrey Shepherd should have
described the poem as growing out of a 'series of illumina-
tions', visionary moments which do not so much convey
thought as challenge it.[4] Shepherd compares these illumina-
tions to the 'showings' of Julian of Norwich. The comparison
is suggestive, even though Langland is not a mystical writer
like Julian (and still less like the author of *The Cloud of
Unknowing*). Thus, one may see in the Piers of Passus XIX–XX
a representation of what Langland found lacking in the
Church of his day; but no analysis or definition of that lack
does justice to the accumulated force of the vision itself. Here,
as in the earlier episode when he tears the pardon, one
recognizes what Woolf calls 'the combination in Piers of
uncertain significance with deep emotional power'.[5]

Shepherd's comparison with Julian of Norwich recalls us to
the question with which this study began, the question of the
unbelieving reader. Can such a reader hope fully to appreciate
the 'deep emotional power' of Langland's poem at those
moments when it touches upon spiritual mysteries? The
answer must be: no, not fully. If one does not believe in the
Incarnation, as the present writer does not, Langland's vision
of the incarnate God 'wearing Piers's arms' may indeed be
understood and admired; but its full force can surely be felt
only by a fellow-believer. Yet *Piers Plowman* is not merely, what
J. A. W. Bennett called it, 'the supreme English testament of
Christian faith'. The eighteenth-century scholar Thomas War-
ton praised its 'strong vein of allegorical invention';[6] and that
prolific 'invention' testifies to the power of the human mind
to create imaginary worlds, within which everyday thoughts

---

[4] 'The Nature of Alliterative Poetry in Late Medieval England', in Shepherd, *Poets
and Prophets: Essays in Medieval Studies*, ed. T. A. Shippey and John Pickles (Cambridge,
1990), 173–92; 189. This Gollancz Memorial Lecture was originally published in
*Proceedings of the British Academy*, 56 (1970), 57–76.

[5] *Art and Doctrine*, 87.

[6] *The History of English Poetry*, rev. edn., 4 vols. (London, 1824), ii. 101.

and feelings may find an expression more vivid and more faithful than ordinary discourse commonly allows. This is the fictive power which helps to explain why Langland's poem can number many unbelievers, as well as many believers, among its devotees.

# Langland and Deguileville:
## *Le Pelerinage de Jhesucrist*

Between about 1330 and about 1360, the French Cistercian Guillaume de Deguileville composed his sequence of three linked pilgrimage poems: *Le Pelerinage de Vie Humaine* (*Vie*) about 1330, revised and expanded about 1355; *Le Pelerinage de l'Ame* (*Ame*) about 1358; and *Le Pelerinage de Jhesucrist* (*Jhesucrist*) some time after 1358.[1] These poems enjoyed a remarkable success. Singly, in pairs, or as a complete trilogy, they survive in more than seventy-five manuscript copies.[2] Evidence for the English production or circulation of these has yet to be studied; but knowledge of Deguileville's work in England is well attested. Chaucer translated his *ABC of the Virgin* from the *Vie*, and Thomas Hoccleve's *Complaint of the Virgin* is from the *Ame*. The English prose translation of the *Ame*, dated 1413, survives in ten manuscripts and was printed by Caxton in 1483; and the prose version of the *Vie* was made at about the same time, surviving in six manuscripts.[3] John Lydgate is the probable author

---

[1] The three poems were all edited by J. J. Stürzinger for the Roxburghe Club: *Le Pelerinage de Vie Humaine de Guillaume de Deguileville* (London, 1893), *Le Pelerinage de l'Ame de Guillaume de Deguileville* (London, 1895), *Le Pelerinage Jhesucrist de Guillaume de Deguileville* (London, 1897). The fullest discussion is by E. Faral, 'Guillaume de Digulleville, Moine de Chaalis', *Histoire Littéraire de la France*, vol. 39 (1962), 1–132. Following Stürzinger, Faral (p. 79) dates the *Jhesucrist* to 1358, on the strength of lines 21–6 in its prologue; but the date given in these lines clearly belongs, not to *Jhesucrist*, but to an earlier poem. The narrator says that he now particularly wants to see the pilgrimage of Christ, because 'en une nuit | L'an mil ccc. lviii. | Songié m'estoie pelerin | Où avoie fait grant chemin, | Et point ne l'avoie veü | En ce chemin ne perceü'. The reference must be to the *Ame*, where the dreamer's post-mortem experiences do indeed not include any sight of Christ. Since Deguileville was already past 60 years old when he wrote the *Ame* (lines 9376–7 there), however, the *Jhesucrist* was itself perhaps written not long after 1358.

[2] So Faral, 'Guillaume de Digulleville', 11. I do not know the exact number. See also Rosemond Tuve, *Allegorical Imagery: Some Mediaeval Books and their Posterity* (Princeton, NJ, 1966), 147 n. 2.

[3] *The Pilgrimage of the Soul: A Critical Edition of the Middle English Dream Vision*, ed. Rosemarie Potz McGurr, vol. i (New York and London, 1990); *The Pilgrimage of the Lyfe of the Manhode*, ed. Avril Henry, EETS 288, 292 (1985, 1988). A French prose version of the *Ame* was made shortly after for John, Duke of Bedford.

of the English verse *Vie*, made in 1426–8; and John Skelton claims to have translated the same work into prose.[4]

A century ago, Jusserand suggested that Langland knew the whole of Deguileville's trilogy, and this opinion was endorsed more recently by Rosemary Woolf.[5] Most students of *Piers Plowman*, however, have concentrated their attention on what was admittedly the most widely read of the set, the *Vie*, to the exclusion of the other two poems.[6] Indeed, the possibility that the last of them, *Jhesucrist*, may have exerted an influence upon the English poet has hardly been explored at all.

It is certainly possible that Langland had access only to the *Vie*, for that poem occurs quite commonly in manuscripts without the other members of the trilogy.[7] Yet there is one consideration in particular which suggests that he did encounter the whole set, or at least more than one member of it. The structuring of *Piers Plowman* as a sequence of dreams linked by waking interludes is one of its most distinctive features; and for this, by far the most likely model is Deguileville's sequence of three dream-pilgrimages.[8] The similarity between the two sequences is necessarily somewhat masked in Stürzinger's editions of the French, where a separate volume is devoted to each poem. Faral, however, reports that, of his 'more than 75' manuscripts, twenty-three contain all three poems in a single volume.[9] Of these, I have seen only the two complete

---

[4] *The Pilgrimage of the Life of Man, Englisht by John Lydgate*, ed. K. B. Locock and F. J. Furnivall, EETS ES 92 (1904); *The Garland of Laurel*, lines 1219–22. Skelton's version has not survived.

[5] J. J. Jusserand, *Piers Plowman: A Contribution to the History of English Mysticism* (London, 1894), 173; Rosemary Woolf, 'The Tearing of the Pardon', in Woolf, *Art and Doctrine*, 139.

[6] The main discussions of *Piers* in relation to the *Vie* are to be found in Dorothy L. Owen's still very useful study, *Piers Plowman: A Comparison with some Earlier and Contemporary French Allegories* (London, 1912; reprinted Norwood Editions, 1978), and in Guy Bourquin, *Piers Plowman: Études sur la genèse littéraire des trois versions* (Lille, Paris, 1978), 780–98. The excellent discussion of Deguileville by Rosemond Tuve, *Allegorical Imagery*, ch. 3, concentrates on the *Vie*, but not in relation to Langland. On *Piers* and the *Ame*, see Owen, *A Comparison*, 124–5, Woolf, 'Tearing of the Pardon', and David Aers, *Piers Plowman and Christian Allegory* (London, 1975), 47–9.

[7] Of his 'more than 75' manuscripts of Deguileville's poems, Faral ('Guillaume de Digulleville', p. 11) reports that 24 have the *Vie* alone.

[8] This was noted by Owen, *A Comparison*, 129: 'The idea of a continuous series of visions may also have been suggested to the writer of "Piers Plowman" by the linking together of De Guileville's three Dream Pilgrimages.' Owen also (pp. 27–9) draws a closer parallel between Deguileville's three dreams and the three dreams of Langland's A Text; but her argument is somewhat strained.

[9] Faral, 'Guillaume de Digulleville', p. 11. For particulars, see Stürzinger's (incomplete) list of MSS in his ed. of the *Vie*, pp. ix–xiii.

Deguilevilles in the British Library and one in the Bodleian Library. British Library MS Additional 38120 concludes each poem with an individual *explicit* ('Explicit le pelerinaige de vie humaine', etc.) and marks them off from each other by blank leaves.[10] In Bodleian Library MS Additional C.29, *Vie* ends at the bottom of the first column of fo. 31$^v$, followed at the top of the second column by 'Amen | Explicit de vie humaine | Et commence Jhesucrist'. The scribe was evidently confused or misled; but, after leaving the rest of the column blank, he begins *Ame* at the top of fo. 32$^r$ with a picture and rubric, 'Cy commence le pelerinage de lame'. *Ame* ends on fo. 110$^r$ with an *explicit*, followed immediately by a picture and rubric, 'Cy commence le pelerinage Jhesucrist'. But the most striking example of a continuous format in these manuscripts is to be seen in British Library MS Additional 22937, in the juncture of *Vie* with *Ame* on fos. 74$^v$–75$^r$. The *Vie* ends with an 'Amen' towards the bottom of the second column of 74$^v$, and is immediately followed there, without any *explicit*, by a rubric which anticipates the pilgrim falling asleep again: 'Comment le pelerin dort en son lit'. This was presumably to have been the subject of the picture occupying the space left at the top of the next leaf; but the illustrator failed to complete this part of the volume. After this space, the text of the *Ame* begins at once, with no *incipit*: 'After I had woken up and marvelled greatly at my dream . . . etc.'[11] Since these words refer to an awakening which occurred at the end of the *Vie*, and make no sense otherwise, it seems that this scribe's treatment of the *Vie–Ame* link is true to the poet's intentions, presenting as it does a continuous sequence: dream, awakening, waking reflections, and falling asleep to dream again.[12] Langland may, of course, have hit upon the idea for himself; but if he did have a source, it was in all probability such a copy of 'Le Roman des trois pelerinages'.

But what evidence is there that Langland knew the latest of Deguileville's dreams, the *Jhesucrist*? Dorothy Owen, almost the only

---

[10] Fo. 110, between *Vie* and *Ame*, contains only an *explicit* and an *incipit*. Between *Ame* and *Jhesucrist*, fos. 197$^v$ and 198 are blank.

[11] A later hand has added the *Ame* title in the blank space left for the illustrator. The junction between *Ame* and *Jhesucrist* is more clearly marked in this manuscript, with an *explicit* and blank spaces on fo. 132$^r$ followed by a rubric at the bottom of the second column introducing the (unexecuted) picture for which space is left at the beginning of fo. 132$^v$. After this space, *Jhesucrist* begins without *incipit*.

[12] A study of the format of all the three-poem Deguileville manuscripts would throw further light on this matter. The printed edition, *Romant des trois pelerinages* (Paris, *c*.1500), treats the three as a continuous sequence. Thus, the wakings of the dreamer after *Vie* and *Ame* are headed 'Reueil premier du pelerin' and 'Reueil second du pelerin' respectively.

scholar to have considered the matter, observed that 'it is especially interesting that each poet should have supplemented his account of human life by relating the Life of our Lord, as seen by him in a vision'.[13] Admittedly, the order of Langland's poem can be compared to that of the French trilogy only in a very general way; but Owen is right also to imply that the very idea of representing the life of Christ in dream form may have been suggested by the *Jhesucrist*, for no other French dream poem takes this as its subject.[14] Although Deguileville follows the course of Christ's life much more systematically and continuously than does Langland, his dream narrative does have certain general features in common with the English poet's. In both, personifications rub shoulders with biblical persons. In the French, Poverty and Nature attend the Nativity, and Ignorance is encountered on the Flight into Egypt, rather as Langland's Faith looks down upon the Entry into Jerusalem (*Jhesucrist* 1819 ff., 3301 ff.; *Piers* XVIII. 15 ff.). In both poems, too, events of Gospel history are seen, as it were, through a dream filter. There is an intervening fictional narrative which determines the presentation of such historical events as can, with more or less plausibility, be represented in its terms. Since Deguileville's master-fiction is that of Christ's life as a pilgrimage, we might have expected Langland, if he knew the French poem, to have adopted this, instead of his more commonplace allegory of Christ as a knight. Yet the Christ-knight theme does play a significant, though secondary, part in the *Jhesucrist*. Deguileville's Christ, as well as being a pilgrim, is also a 'chevalier et champion' (line 3350), destined to fight against Death and Satan (5021–23). He enters Jerusalem on Palm Sunday as a warrior, albeit without saddle or armour (7583–90); and on the cross his side is pierced by the lance of a 'chevalier', Longeus (9643–45).[15]

Where a motif is as widely current as that of the Christ-knight, such parallels are of limited significance; but one other passage in Deguileville's version anticipates Langland more closely. When the Holy Family, on their flight or 'pilgrimage' to Egypt, encounter Ignorance, he scornfully asks Jesus why such a 'chevalier et champion', already 'vestu et armé' by his mother, should be running away from his enemy (3319–56). Joseph replies on behalf of the infant. Jesus has indeed come to fight as a champion against his adversary Death (3374–78); but he needs time to learn the arts of war:

[13] *A Comparison*, 20.
[14] Grosseteste's *Chateau d'Amour*, which Langland may have known, does treat the life of Christ, but is not a dream poem.
[15] See also lines 6422, 8931, 10565–72.

> N'est champion qui aprendre
> D'envär et soi deffendre
> Ne doie, avant quë il aille
> En champ -mortel pour bataille.[16]

His time has not yet come, and he still has much to learn:

> Quar n'est mie le tempz venu
> Que doie encor estre vëu
> En guerre ne en bataille
> Qui' apris rien encor sanz faille
> N'en a, et faut que par lonc tempz
> De ce faire ait ensegnemens,
> Et qu'il croisse et deviegne grant
> En delaissant l'estat d'enfant,
> Et en prenant autre guise
> Quë u ciel n'a pas aprise
> Où onques forz païz il ne vit.          (3431–41)

The parallel here is with *Piers* XVI. 103–7, the passage discussed in Chapter 3 (p. 74 above), where Piers Plowman 'parceyved plener tyme' and in the meanwhile taught the child Jesus the knightly arts of surgery. It is striking that both poets should apply the Christ-knight theme to the particular problem of why the incarnate God spent so long on earth before starting to tackle his mission: like a young knight learning the skills of chivalry, Jesus needed time to learn as a man 'what he had not learned in heaven'.[17]

Not all the parallels between *Piers* and the *Jhesucrist* concern the Christ-knight. There remain, in particular, striking similarities in the ways the two poets begin and end their dream of Christ's life. As already noted in Chapter 3 (pp. 54–5 above), Deguileville's *Vita Christi* is prefaced by a vision of an apple tree. An old man, later identified as Adam, climbs the tree and eats the fruit; but he loses his footing, and the earth opens to receive him as he falls (lines 65–74). This event prompts discussion in heaven, which in turn leads to the Annunciation. Langland's sequence in XVI. 73–91 may be regarded as an abbreviated,

---

[16] Lines 3381–4. God the Father makes a similar point to the Holy Spirit later, on the occasion of Christ's baptism: 'Si est tempz que doie aprendre | A assallir et defendre | Soi, et quë ait premierement | Touz les tours d'escremissement' (5025–28).

[17] In a similar passage, XIX. 96–107, where Langland's Conscience speaks of the young Jesus learning the many 'sleightes' that a conqueror has to master, there is a curious reference to his fleeing: 'And som tyme he faught faste, and fleigh outherwhile' (103). This has been explained as an allusion to King David's guerrilla tactics: T. D. Hill, *Notes and Queries*, 221 (1976), 291–4; but a better explanation is to be found in the *Jhesucrist*, where the discussion between Ignorance and Joseph makes several references to Jesus 'fleeing' into Egypt: lines 3315, 3334, 3340, 3352, etc.

speeded-up version of this same tree–fall–incarnation sequence. Certainly his Tree of Charity, from which Adam and the rest 'dropped adoun', has exactly the same part to play as Deguileville's apple tree, in providing a visionary prologue to the Annunciation.[18] Even more striking is the similarity, already noted in Chapter 1, between the close of Deguileville's dream and that of Langland's dream of the Harrowing of Hell. The celebrations which attend Christ's triumphant return from Hell in *Piers* XVIII. 408–28 closely resemble the heavenly rejoicings which, in the *Jhesucrist*, greet his Ascension and the Assumption of Mary. At the Ascension, Justice, Mercy, and Truth embrace and kiss (10471–75: Deguileville commonly has only three Daughters of God); and there follows a great festival to celebrate the Son's return, at which all the three Daughters sing in turn and are joined by a mass chorus of angels and spirits. At the Assumption of the Virgin the celebrations are renewed. The heavenly hosts join with Gabriel in a great 'nouvel chant' to mark the return of Christ and his mother; and the sound of this song, with its accompaniment of heavenly instruments, wakens the dreamer:

> Un songe fu, si com tost vi,
> Quar par le grant son quë oui
> Et par la chanterie grant
> Toutes mez orelles remplant
> Esvellié fu . . .                    (11197–201)

Here once more Langland's vision may be seen as a condensation of Deguileville's, combining the Daughters of God and their embraces with the 'chanterie grant' and instrumental music which wake Will, as they also woke Guillaume.

No one of these parallels is in itself decisive evidence; yet they surely serve to fortify the position taken by Rosemary Woolf: 'Langland probably knew Guillaume's trilogy, for it contains so many possible sources for individual allegories in *Piers Plowman*, and even for the outline structure of the wandering pilgrim, that it would be a strong coincidence if Langland had gathered the allegories that he has in common with Guillaume from other scattered sources.'[19]

---

[18] The parallel is discussed in Michelle Martindale, 'The Treatment of the Life of Christ in *Piers Plowman*', B.Litt. thesis (Oxford, 1978), 17–19.

[19] 'The Tearing of the Pardon', 139. I note here a number of other, miscellaneous parallels between *Jhesucrist* and *Piers*: a vision of the world from a mountain, *Jhesucrist* 92–108, *Piers* XI. 323–71; Christ's incognito, *Jhesucrist* 951–71, 1091–100, 5035–44, *Piers* XVIII. 22–6, 296–7; Christ in Mary's 'chamber', *Jhesucrist* 1235, *Piers* XVI. 92; the marriage garment of the soul laundered by penance, *Jhesucrist* 5941–8, *Piers* XIV. 1–21; Christ seeing men's thoughts, *Jhesucrist* 7288, 7717–36, *Piers* XV. 199–212; Christ's thirst for man's salvation, *Jhesucrist* 9421–34, *Piers* XVIII. 366–71.

APPENDIX B.

# Piers Plowman and Saint Peter:
## B XV. 195–212

In the text above, pp. 77–80, I discussed the relationship which develops in Passus XIX and XX of the B Text between Piers Plowman and St Peter. There can be no question of reading back into the whole poem any general identification between Langland's hero and the apostle. The most that can be said in general is that the plowman and the fisherman do have features in common. They are both 'homines sine litteris et idiotae', 'illiterate and ignorant men', as Acts 4: 13 says of Peter and John; and they both on occasion act with impulsive violence.[1] So it is at least not inappropriate that the first word spoken by Piers in the poem should be 'Peter': ' "Peter!" quod a plowman, and putte forth his hed' (V. 537). However, there is only one place, before Passus XIX, where Piers is explicitly associated with the historical Peter. This occurs in the course of Anima's discussion of charity—a virtue which Will expresses a desire to 'know':

'By Crist! I wolde that I knewe hym,' quod I, 'no creature levere!'
'Withouten help of Piers Plowman,' quod he, 'his persone
  sestow nevere.'
'Wheither clerkes knowen hym,' quod I, 'that kepen Holi Kirke?'
'Clerkes have no knowyng,' quod he, 'but by werkes and by wordes.
Ac Piers the Plowman parceyveth moore depper
What is the wille, and wherfore that many wight suffreth:

---

[1] Cf. Murtaugh's observation on B XIX. 321–2: 'When Piers speaks with such rough practicality to Grace we recognize the hurried, efficient foreman of the half-acre. We recognize, too, for the first time, that these tones are perfectly appropriate to the bluff, impulsive fisherman of the Gospels', D. M. Murtaugh, *'Piers Plowman' and the Image of God* (Gainesville, Fla., 1978), 59. The violent 'tene' with which Piers tears the pardon (VII. 115) and throws a stick at the scrumping Devil (XVI. 86) might be compared with Peter's angry action in cutting off the ear of the high priest's servant (John 18: 10); and the refusal by Piers to accept money in return for guiding the people on their pilgrimage (V. 556–9) certainly resembles the response of Peter to Simon Magus: 'Keep thy money to thyself to perish with thee: because thou hast thought that the gift of God may be purchased with money' (Acts 8: 20). This latter resemblance is noted by Margaret E. Goldsmith, in the course of a valuable discussion of the relationship between Piers and Peter: *The Figure of Piers Plowman: The Image on the Coin* (Cambridge, 1981), 31.

*Et vidit Deus cogitaciones eorum.*
For ther are ful proude herted men, pacient of tonge
And buxome as of berynge to burgeises and to lordes,
And to poore peple han pepir in the nose,
And as a lyoun he loketh ther men lakken hise werkes.
For ther are beggeris and bidderis, bedemen as it were,
Loken as lambren and semen lif-holy—
Ac it is moore to have hir mete on swich an esy manere
Than for penaunce and parfitnesse, the poverte that
    swiche taketh.
Therfore by colour ne by clergie knowe shaltow hym nevere,
Neither thorugh wordes ne werkes, but thorugh wil oone,
And that knoweth no clerk ne creature on erthe
But Piers the Plowman—*Petrus, id est, Christus.*'

(XV. 195–212)

Discussion of this passage, and especially of the concluding '*Petrus, id est, Christus*', has sometimes been obscured by a failure to recognize its rather specific point. Anima takes Will's expressed desire to 'know charity' as raising the question of moral judgement. How, that is, can one be sure about the true moral condition of another person? For, as Anima points out, what people say and what they do, their 'wordes' and their 'werkes', commonly fail to represent their true intentions, their 'wil'.[2] So the only really safe way of arriving at a moral judgement, Anima says, is to see directly into people's minds and hearts, and thus bypass the unreliable evidences of word and deed. This is what God is able to do: '*Et vidit Deus cogitaciones eorum*', 'And God saw their thoughts'. Anima here recalls a number of passages in the Gospels where Jesus is said to see or know the thoughts of others.[3] In displaying this strange power, Jesus fulfilled the messianic prophecy of Isaiah: 'He shall not judge according to the sight of the eyes [*werkes*], nor reprove according to the hearing of the ears [*wordes*].'[4]

[2] I took no account of St Peter in my earlier discussion: 'Words, Works and Will: Theme and Structure in *Piers Plowman*', in S. S. Hussey (ed.), *Piers Plowman: Critical Approaches* (London, 1969), 111–24.

[3] Anima's quotation resembles Matt. 9: 4, where Jesus confronts the scribes: 'Et cum vidisset Jesus cogitationes eorum, dixit . . . '. Similar expressions are used in Matt. 12: 25, and Luke 5: 22, 6: 8, 9: 47, 11: 17. The same quotation occurs in the corresponding passage in the C Text, XVI. 336–9 (where, however, the argument is confused by allowing that charity *can* be known from 'werkes'). James Simpson refers in this connection to Augustine's *De Trinitate*: ' "Et vidit deus cogitationes eorum": A Parallel Instance and Possible Source for Langland's Use of a Biblical Formula at *Piers Plowman* B XV. 200a', *Notes and Queries*, 231 (1986), 9–13.

[4] Isa. 11: 3. This forms part of the famous Jesse prophecy. It follows immediately

However, Anima does not suggest that this power died with Jesus. It can still be exercised today—but only with the help of Piers Plowman, who 'parceyveth moore depper | What is the wille, and wherfore that many wight suffreth'. The fact that this claim for Piers is supported first by the Gospel quotation about God and later by the flat statement '*Petrus, id est, Christus*' has led some readers, understandably enough, to see here a direct equation between Piers and *Deus* or *Christus*; but the matter cannot be as simple as that, for the '*Petrus*' of line 212 introduces a third party into the argument, St Peter. The prime source of Anima's words here is to be found in St Paul's allegorization of the experiences of the Israelites in the wilderness; according to Paul, the rock from which Moses struck water is to be understood as Christ: 'petra autem erat Christus', 'and the rock was Christ' (1 Corinthians 10: 4). But Anima's substitution of *Petrus* for *petra* in his version depends upon Christ's punning promise to St Peter: 'tu es Petrus, et super hanc petram aedificabo ecclesiam meam', 'thou art Peter, and upon this rock I will build my church' (Matthew 16: 18). So the effect of Langland's line 212, taken as a whole, is to link Piers with Peter first, and only then with Christ—and that, one must presume, only in respect of the power in question, that of directly 'knowing the will'.

We have here, I believe, further evidence of Langland's drawing upon the Acts of the Apostles.[5] There, in the strange episode of Ananias and Saphira, Peter is shown in the act of exerting precisely the same Christlike power that Anima attributes to Piers (Acts 5: 1–10). Having sold a piece of land, Ananias brings only part of the proceeds to the apostles: 'But Peter said: Ananias, why hath Satan tempted thy heart, that thou shouldst lie to the Holy Ghost and by fraud keep part of the price of the land? . . . Why hast thou conceived this thing in thy heart? Thou hast not lied to men, but to God.' A modern reader may see nothing in this but apostolic shrewdness—Peter is a good judge of men—but medieval readers saw it otherwise. Thus Peter Comestor, in his *Historia Scholastica*, writes as follows of Ananias' deceit: 'Quod statim Petrus praevidens in Spiritu ait: "Anania, cur tentavit Satanas cor tuum mentiri te Spiritui sancto? Cur fraudasti de pretio agri? Non es mentitus hominibus sed Deo", qui scrutatur corda, et perdit omnes qui loquuntur mendacium.'[6] So Peter is able to see through the deceitful

after the verses concerning the gifts of the Holy Spirit which Langland draws on, in connection with Piers, in Passus XIX (see pp. 68–9 above). It provides the likely inspiration for the poet's thinking about words and actions as indices of a moral state.

[5] See above, pp. 79–80.
[6] 'Perceiving this immediately in the Spirit, Peter said: "Ananias, why hath Satan

Ananias by virtue of his power of spiritual vision ('praevidens in Spiritu'), a power derived from that God 'qui scrutatur corda, et perdit omnes qui loquuntur mendacium'.[7]

Though the Peter–Piers of Passus XIX does not display this power, it is entirely in keeping with the poet's exalted conception of him as the Holy Spirit's chief representative on earth. Significantly, it is in the absence of Piers at the end of the poem that Conscience proves incapable of seeing through the deceitful behaviour of the friars, and so admits them into the barn Unity. Even Conscience is no *scrutator cordis*. Yet Anima's remarks suggest that even today a latter-day Peter, one who shares with the apostle in Christ's spiritual legacy, may prove worthy of inheriting that prophetic ability to see men's thoughts which Jesus displayed in his lifetime.[8]

tempted thy heart, that thou shouldst lie to the Holy Ghost? Why hast thou by fraud kept part of the price of the land? Thou hast not lied to men, but to God", who searches hearts and destroys all those that speak a lie': Comestor, *Historia Scholastica*, *PL* 198.1659. The significance of the Ananias episode was noted by Margaret Goldsmith, *Figure of Piers Plowman*, 35–6. Among the spiritual gifts of prophecy in the primitive Church, St Paul includes the power of perceiving *occulta cordis*: 'But if all prophesy, and there come in one that believeth not or an unlearned person, he is convinced of all: he is judged of all. The secrets of his heart are made manifest. And so, falling down on his face, he will adore God, affirming that God is among you indeed', 1 Cor. 14: 24–5. St Gregory, quoting this passage in his discussion of prophecy, counts knowledge of 'thought hidden in the secret heart' as one example of *prophetia de praesenti* (prophetic knowledge of a present, as against a past or a future, fact): *Homiliarum in Ezechielem Prophetam Libri Duo*, *PL* 76.787.

[7] Comestor's added reference to God *qui scrutatur corda* recalls Old Testament passages where God's ability to see into thoughts and hearts is alluded to: 'Consumetur nequitia peccatorum; et diriges justum, scrutans corda et renes, Deus', 'The wickedness of sinners shall be brought to nought, and thou shalt direct the just: the searcher of hearts and reins is God' (Ps. 7: 10, AV 7: 9); 'omnia enim corda scrutatur Dominus, et universas mentium cogitationes intelligit', 'for the Lord searcheth all hearts, and understandeth all the thoughts of minds' (1 Chron. 28: 9).

[8] The same conclusion is stated by Robertson and Huppé: 'Christ established the power of apostolic discernment into the hearts of men. This function of his divinity he transmitted to Peter, and through him to his successors. As part of the apostolic tradition, it is a function of Piers Plowman; in so far as Christ and Piers share this power, they are the same', D. W. Robertson, Jr., and Bernard F. Huppé, *Piers Plowman and Scriptural Tradition* (Princeton, NJ, 1951), 183. Similarly E. T. Donaldson, *Piers Plowman: The C-Text and its Poet* (New Haven, Conn., 1949), 185, citing Konrad Burdach, *Der Dichter des Ackermann aus Böhmen und seine Zeit*: vol. iii, pt. 2 of Burdach's *Vom Mittelalter zur Reformation* (Berlin, 1926–32), 311–12.

# Select Bibliography

PRIMARY SOURCES

ARATOR, *De Actibus Apostolorum*, ed. A. P. McKinley (Corpus Scriptorum Ecclesiasticorum Latinorum, 72; Vienna, 1951).

*The Book of Vices and Virtues*, ed. W. Nelson Francis (EETS 217; 1942).

BOZON, NICHOLAS, *Du roi ki avait une amye*, ed. T. Wright, in *The Chronicle of Pierre de Langtoft*, vol. ii (Rolls Series; London, 1868).

*The Castle of Perseverance*, ed. Mark Eccles (EETS 262; 1969).

DEGUILEVILLE, GUILLAUME DE, *Le Pelerinage de Vie Humaine*, ed. J. J. Stürzinger (Roxburghe Club; London, 1893).

—— *The Pilgrimage of the Lyfe of the Manhode*, ed. Avril Henry, 2 vols. (EETS 288, 292; 1985, 1988).

—— *Le Pelerinage de l'Ame*, ed. J. J. Stürzinger (Roxburghe Club; London, 1895).

—— *The Pilgrimage of the Soul: A Critical Edition of the Middle English Dream Vision*, ed. Rosemarie Potz McGurr, vol. i (New York and London, 1990).

—— *Le Pelerinage Jhesucrist*, ed. J. J. Stürzinger (Roxburghe Club; London, 1897).

—— *Romant des trois pelerinages* (Paris, *c*.1500).

GROSSETESTE, ROBERT, *Le Chateau d'Amour de Robert Grosseteste, évèque de Lincoln*, ed. J. Murray (Paris, 1918).

—— *The Middle English Translations of Robert Grosseteste's 'Chateau d'Amour'*, ed. Kari Sajavaara (Mémoires de la Société Néophilologique de Helsinki, 32; 1967).

*L'Histoire de Guillaume le Maréchal*, ed. P. Meyer (Paris, 1891–1901).

ISIDORE OF SEVILLE, *Etymologiae*, ed. W. M. Lindsay (Oxford, 1911).

LANGLAND, WILLIAM, *Piers Plowman: The A Version*, ed. George Kane (London, 1960).

—— *The Vision of Piers Plowman: A Complete Edition of the B-Text*, ed. A. V. C. Schmidt, rev. edn. (London, 1987).

—— *Piers Plowman: The B Version*, ed. George Kane and E. Talbot Donaldson (London, 1975).

—— *Piers Plowman, by William Langland: An Edition of the C-Text*, ed. Derek Pearsall (London, 1978).

—— *The Vision of William Concerning Piers the Plowman in Three Parallel Texts*, ed. W. W. Skeat, 2 vols. (Oxford, 1886).

LORRIS, GUILLAUME DE, and JEAN DE MEUN, *Le Roman de la Rose*, ed. Félix Lecoy (Classiques Français du Moyen Age; Paris, 1965–70).

MERI, HUON DE, *Li Tornoiemenz Antecrit*, ed. Georg Wimmer (Marburg, 1888).

PETRARCH, *Secretum*, ed. Enrico Carrara, in *Francesco Petrarca, Prose*, ed. G. Martellotti, P. G. Ricci, E. Carrara, and E. Bianchi (Milan and Naples, 1955).

RUTEBEUF, *Œuvres complètes*, ed. Michel Zink, vol. i (Paris, 1989).

SERVIUS, *Servianorum in Vergilii Carmina Commentariorum*, ed. E. K. Rand and others (Special Publications of the American Philological Association, no. 1, vol. ii; Lancaster, Pa., 1946).

*Le Songe de Paradis*, ed. A. Scheler, in *Trouvères Belges*, nouvelle série (Louvain, 1879).


SECONDARY SOURCES


ADAMS, ROBERT, 'The Nature of Need in *Piers Plowman* XX', *Traditio*, 34 (1978), 273–301.

—— 'The Reliability of the Rubrics in the B-Text of *Piers Plowman*', *Medium Aevum*, 54 (1985), 208–31.

AERS, DAVID, *Piers Plowman and Christian Allegory* (London, 1975).

—— *Chaucer, Langland and the Creative Imagination* (London, 1980).

—— *Community, Gender, and Individual Identity: English Writing 1360–1430* (London, 1988).

ALFORD, JOHN A., 'Literature and Law in Medieval England', *PMLA* 92 (1977), 941–51.

—— *Piers Plowman: A Glossary of Legal Diction* (Cambridge, 1988).

AMES, RUTH M., *The Fulfillment of the Scriptures: Abraham, Moses, and Piers* (Evanston, Ill., 1970).

BALDWIN, ANNA P., 'The Double Duel in Piers Plowman B XVIII and C XXI', *Medium Aevum*, 50 (1981), 64–78.

BARNEY, STEPHEN A., 'The Plowshare of the Tongue: The Progress of a Symbol from the Bible to *Piers Plowman*', *Mediaeval Studies*, 35 (1973), 261–93.

—— *Allegories of History, Allegories of Love* (Hamden, Conn., 1979).

BARTHES, ROLAND, *S/Z* (Paris, 1970).

BENNETT, J. A. W., *Poetry of the Passion: Studies in Twelve Centuries of English Verse* (Oxford, 1982).

BENSON, C. DAVID, 'An Augustinian Irony in *Piers Plowman*', *Notes and Queries*, 221 (1976), 51–4.

BIRNES, WILLIAM J., 'Christ as Advocate: The Legal Metaphor of *Piers Plowman*', *Annuale Mediaevale*, 16 (1975), 71–93.

BLOOMFIELD, MORTON W., *Piers Plowman as a Fourteenth-Century Apocalypse* (New Brunswick, NJ, n.d. [1961]).

BOURQUIN, GUY, *Piers Plowman: Études sur la genèse littéraire des trois versions* (Lille, Paris, 1978).

BURDACH, KONRAD, *Vom Mittelalter zur Reformation* (Berlin, 1926–32).

BURROW, J. A., 'The Action of Langland's Second Vision', *Essays in Criticism*, 15 (1965), 247–68.

—— 'Words, Works and Will: Theme and Structure in *Piers Plowman*', in S. S. Hussey (ed.), *Piers Plowman: Critical Approaches* (London, 1969), 111–24.

—— 'Langland *Nel Mezzo del Cammin*', in P. L. Heyworth (ed.), *Medieval Studies for J. A. W. Bennett* (Oxford, 1981), 21–41.

—— *Medieval Writers and their Work* (Oxford, 1982).

—— *Essays on Medieval Literature* (Oxford, 1984).

——'Autobiographical Poetry in the Middle Ages: The Case of Thomas Hoccleve', in J. A. Burrow (ed.), *Middle English Literature: British Academy Gollancz Lectures* (Oxford, 1989), 223–46.

CARRUTHERS, MARY J., *The Search for St. Truth: A Study of Meaning in Piers Plowman* (Evanston, Ill., 1973).

—— 'Time, Apocalypse, and the Plot of *Piers Plowman*', in M. J. Carruthers and E. D. Kirk (eds.), *Acts of Interpretation: The Text in its Contexts 700–1600. Essays on Medieval and Renaissance Literature in Honor of E. Talbot Donaldson* (Norman, Okla., 1982), 175–88.

CHAMBERS, R. W., *Man's Unconquerable Mind* (London, 1939).

CHATMAN, SEYMOUR, *Story and Discourse: Narrative Structure in Fiction and Film* (Ithaca, NY, 1978).

CULLMANN, OSCAR, *Peter: Disciple–Apostle–Martyr*, trans. Floyd V. Filson (London, 1953).

DAVLIN, M. C., '*Kynde Knowynge* as a Major Theme in *Piers Plowman* B', *Review of English Studies*, NS 22 (1971), 1–19.

DONALDSON, E. TALBOT, *Piers Plowman: The C-Text and its Poet* (New Haven, Conn., 1949).

—— 'Long Will's Apology: A Translation', in Gregory Kratzmann and James Simpson (eds.), *Medieval English Religious and Ethical Literature: Essays in Honour of G. H. Russell* (Cambridge, 1986), 30–4.

EAKIN, PAUL JOHN, *Fictions in Autobiography: Studies in the Art of Self-Invention* (Princeton, NJ. 1985).

ELBAZ, ROBERT, *The Changing Nature of the Self: A Critical Study of the Autobiographical Discourse* (London, 1988).

FRANK, R. W., 'The Number of Visions in *Piers Plowman*', *Modern Language Notes*, 66 (1951), 309–12.

—— *Piers Plowman and the Scheme of Salvation* (New Haven, Conn., 1957).

——— 'The "Hungry Gap", Crop Failure, and Famine: The Four-teenth-Century Agricultural Crisis and *Piers Plowman*', *Yearbook of Langland Studies*, 4 (1990), 87–104.

GAFFNEY, WILBUR, 'The Allegory of the Christ-Knight in *Piers Plowman*', *PMLA* 46 (1931), 155–68.

GENETTE, GÉRARD, *Narrative Discourse*, trans. J. E. Lewin (Oxford, 1980).

GODDEN, MALCOLM, *The Making of Piers Plowman* (London, 1990).

GOFFMAN, ERVING, *The Presentation of Self in Everyday Life* (Harmondsworth, 1969).

GOLDSMITH, MARGARET E., *The Figure of Piers Plowman: The Image on the Coin* (Cambridge, 1981).

HARBERT, BRUCE, 'Langland's Easter', in Helen Phillips (ed.), *Langland, the Mystics and the Medieval English Religious Tradition: Essays in Honour of S. S. Hussey* (Cambridge, 1990), 57–70.

HIEATT, CONSTANCE B., *The Realism of Dream Visions: The Poetic Exploitation of the Dream-Experience in Chaucer and his Contemporaries* (The Hague and Paris, 1967).

JUNG, MARC-RENÉ, *Études sur le poème allégorique en France au Moyen Age* (Berne, 1971).

KANE, GEORGE, *Piers Plowman: The Evidence for Authorship* (London, 1965).

——— *Chaucer and Langland: Historical and Textual Approaches* (London, 1989).

KERBY-FULTON, KATHRYN, *Reformist Apocalypticism and Piers Plowman* (Cambridge, 1990).

KRUGER, STEVEN F., *Dreaming in the Middle Ages* (Cambridge, 1992).

LAWTON, DAVID, 'The Subject of *Piers Plowman*', *Yearbook of Langland Studies*, 1 (1987), 1–30.

MARTINDALE, MICHELLE, 'The Treatment of the Life of Christ in *Piers Plowman*', B.Litt. thesis (Oxford, 1978).

MIDDLETON, ANNE, 'Narration and the Invention of Experience: Episodic Form in *Piers Plowman*', in L. D. Benson and S. Wenzel (eds.), *The Wisdom of Poetry: Essays in Early English Literature in Honor of Morton W. Bloomfield* (Kalamazoo, Mich., 1982), 91–122.

——— 'William Langland's "Kynde Name": Authorial Signature and Social Identity in Late Fourteenth-Century England', in Lee Patterson (ed.), *Literary Practice and Social Change in Britain*, 1380–1530 (Berkeley, Calif., 1990), 15–82.

MITCHELL, A. G., 'Lady Meed and the Art of *Piers Plowman*', in R. J. Blanch (ed.), *Style and Symbolism in Piers Plowman: A Modern Critical Anthology* (Knoxville, Tenn., 1969), 174–93.

MURTAUGH, DANIEL M., *Piers Plowman and the Image of God* (Gainesville, Fla., 1978).

OLNEY, JAMES (ed.), *Autobiography: Essays Theoretical and Critical* (Princeton, NJ, 1980).

OLSON, GLENDING, *Literature as Recreation in the Later Middle Ages* (Ithaca, NY, 1982).

OVERSTREET, SAMUEL A., 'Langland's Elusive Plowman', *Traditio*, 45 (1989–90), 257–341.

OWEN, DOROTHY L., *Piers Plowman: A Comparison with some Earlier and Contemporary French Allegories* (London, 1912; reprinted 1978).

PEARSALL, DEREK, 'Poverty and Poor People in *Piers Plowman*', in Edward John Kennedy, Ronald Waldron, and Joseph S. Wittig (eds.), *Medieval English Studies Presented to George Kane* (Woodbridge, 1988), 167–85.

REED, THOMAS L., *Middle English Debate Poetry and the Aesthetics of Irresolution* (Columbia, Mo., 1990).

ROBERTSON, D. W., Jr., and HUPPÉ, B. F., *Piers Plowman and Scriptural Tradition* (Princeton, NJ, 1951).

RUBIN, DAVID C. (ed.), *Autobiographical Memory* (Cambridge, 1986).

SAINT-JACQUES, RAYMOND, 'Langland's Christ-Knight and the Liturgy', *Revue de l'Université d'Ottawa*, 37 (1967), 146–58.

SAMUELS, M. L., 'Langland's Dialect', *Medium Aevum*, 54 (1985), 232–47.

SCASE, WENDY, *Piers Plowman and the New Anticlericalism* (Cambridge, 1989).

SHEPHERD, GEOFFREY, 'The Nature of Alliterative Poetry in Late Medieval England', in his *Poets and Prophets: Essays in Medieval Studies*, ed. T. A. Shippey and John Pickles (Cambridge, 1990), 173–92.

SIMPSON, JAMES, ' "Et vidit deus cogitaciones eorum": A Parallel Instance and Possible Source for Langland's Use of a Biblical Formula at *Piers Plowman* B XV. 200a', *Notes and Queries*, 231 (1986), 9–13.

—— *Piers Plowman: An Introduction to the B-Text* (London, 1990).

SPEARING, A. C., *Medieval Dream-Poetry* (Cambridge, 1976).

STOKES, MYRA, *Justice and Mercy in Piers Plowman: A Reading of the B Text Visio* (London, 1984).

SZITTYA, PENN R., *The Antifraternal Tradition in Medieval Literature* (Princeton, NJ, 1986).

TAYLOR, CHARLES, *Sources of the Self: The Making of the Modern Identity* (Cambridge, 1989).

TRAVER, HOPE, *The Four Daughters of God* (Philadelphia, 1907).

TRIMPI, WESLEY, *Muses of One Mind: The Literary Analysis of Experience and its Continuity* (Princeton, NJ, 1983).

TUVE, ROSEMOND, *Allegorical Imagery: Some Mediaeval Books and their Posterity* (Princeton, NJ, 1966).

VAN DYKE, CAROLYNN, *The Fiction of Truth: Structures of Meaning in Narrative and Dramatic Allegory* (Ithaca, NY, 1985).

VAUGHAN, M. F., 'The Liturgical Perspectives of *Piers Plowman* B XVI–XIX', *Studies in Medieval and Renaissance History*, 3 (1980), 87–155.

WALDRON, R. A., 'Langland's Originality: The Christ-Knight and the Harrowing of Hell', in Gregory Kratzmann and James Simpson (eds.), *Medieval English Religious and Ethical Literature: Essays in Honour of G. H. Russell* (Cambridge, 1986), 66–81.

WARTON, THOMAS, *The History of English Poetry*, rev. edn., 4 vols. (London, 1824).

WHITE, HAYDEN, *Metahistory: The Historical Imagination in Nineteenth-Century Europe* (Baltimore and London, 1973).

WITTIG, JOSEPH S., '*Piers Plowman* B, Passus IX–XII: Elements in the Design of the Inward Journey', *Traditio*, 28 (1972), 211–80.

WOOLF, ROSEMARY, 'Some Non-Medieval Qualities of *Piers Plowman*', in her *Art and Doctrine: Essays on Medieval Literature*, ed. Heather O'Donoghue (London, 1986), 85–97.

—— 'The Tearing of the Pardon', in her *Art and Doctrine*, 131–56.

YUNCK, JOHN A., *The Lineage of Lady Meed* (Notre Dame, Ind., 1963).

ZIMMERMAN, T. C. PRICE, 'Confession and Autobiography in the Early Renaissance', in Anthony Molho and John A. Tedeschi (eds.), *Renaissance: Studies in Honor of Hans Baron* (Dekalb, Ill., and Florence, 1971), 119–40.

ZINK, MICHEL, *La Subjectivité littéraire: Autour du siècle de Saint Louis* (Paris, 1985).

# Index

Abraham 56, 58, 63, 64–5, 80, 82
Adams, Robert 20 n.
Aers, David 35 n.
Ames, Ruth M. 59
Ananias and Saphira 121–2
Anima 118–22
Aquinas, Thomas, *Summa Theologica* 29,
  70, 105
Arator, *De Actibus Apostolorum* 68, 70 n.
Augustine, St, *Confessions* 87

Barthes, Roland, *S/Z* 10 n.
Bennett, J. A. W. 1, 111
*Bestiaire de Gervaise* 61
Bible:
  Acts of the Apostles 56, 67–8, 79–
    80, 119, 121–2
  Apocalypse (Revelation) 36, 57 n.
  Corinthians 68, 121, 122 n.
  Isaiah 16, 30, 66 n., 69, 76–7, 120
  Job 32, 98 n.
  John, Epistle of 92
  John, Gospel of 77–8, 118 n.
  Luke 40, 43, 63, 65, 97 n., 120 n.
  Matthew 48, 78, 104, 120 n., 121
  Psalms 30–1, 33, 57 n., 122 n.
  Romans 56
  Thessalonians 42, 43
  Timothy 57, 71
Bloom, Harold 74
Boethius, *Consolatio Philosophiae* 30
*Book of Vices and Virtues* 69
Bozon, Nicholas, *Du roi ki avait une
  amye* 72–3
Bunyan, John, *Pilgrim's Progress* 58–9
Burley, Simon 73

Calote (Will's daughter) 83, 84, 86 n.
Calvino, Italo, *If on a Winter's Night a
  Traveller* 9
Carruthers, Mary J. 9 n.
*Castle of Perseverance* 30, 34
Cato, Dionysius, *Disticha* 28, 42 n., 94
Chaucer, Geoffrey 2, 6, 28
  *ABC of the Virgin* 113
  *Book of the Duchess* 6, 13
  *Canterbury Tales* 2, 34–5, 55 n., 93

*House of Fame* 6, 83
*Troilus and Criseyde* 2, 7, 25
Clergy 3–4, 47, 50–2, 110
*Cloud of Unknowing* 111
Coleridge, S. T. 58–9
Comestor, Peter, *Historia Scholastica*
  121–2
Conscience 10, 13, 15, 17–18, 25–6,
  38–40, 66, 77–8
  as dinner host 3, 22, 44, 47, 49–52,
    110
  and Will 96–9, 100, 104–6, 107

Dante 56, 74
Deguileville, Guillaume de 6, 8
  *Pelerinage de l'Ame* 14, 30, 60, 113, 115
  *Pelerinage de Jhesucrist* 14, 16, 30, 54–
    5, 59, 60, 72, 113–18
  *Pelerinage de Vie Humaine* 14, 17, 60,
    114, 115
  *see also* Lydgate, *Pilgrimage of the Lyfe
    of the Manhode*, *Pilgrimage of the Soul*
Donaldson, E. T. 29, 86
*Dream of the Rood* 61
Dryden, John, *Absalom and Achitophel* 80
Dunbar, William, *The Golden Targe* 13

Eliot, T. S. 3

Faith, Hope, and Charity 22–3, 24,
  56, 81
Four Daughters of God 9–10, 16, 30–
  4, 67, 118
Freud, Sigmund 6
Frye, Northrop 82

Genette, Gérard, *Narrative Discourse*
  20 n., 57–8, 62
Gornemans de Gorhaut 74
Grosseteste, Robert, *Chateau d'Amour*
  66 n., 67 n., 79–80, 116 n.
Guillaume de Lorris, see *Roman de la
  Rose*

Hoccleve, Thomas 84, 113
Hugh of St Victor, *Summa Sententiarum*
  69–70

DATE DUE